PETER KNIGHT was born in
in Cheltenham, Sierra Leone
Royal West African Frontier
Hampstead, NW3. He is married and lives in a small
mediaeval town in central France.

TRAVELS WITH A BRIEFCASE

Odd fragments of a working life

Peter Knight

SilverWood

Cover images:
map Dreamstime © Cornishman
luggage tag iStockphoto © Sudhir Karnataki

Published in paperback by SilverWood Books 2010
www.silverwoodbooks.co.uk

ISBN 978-1-906236-45-8

British Library Cataloguing in Publication Data
A CIP catalogue record for this book is available from the British Library

Set in 11pt Sabon by SilverWood Books
Printed in England on paper from sustainable sources

I travelled among unknown men,
In lands beyond the sea;
Nor England! Did I know till then
What love I bore to thee.

William Wordsworth 1770–1850

Travel, in the younger sort, is a part of education;
in the elder, a part of experience.

Francis Bacon 1561–1626: *Of Travel*

To Oliver, Jessica and Sidonie

Contents

Acknowledgements

First I wish to recognise the contribution made by the readers of my initial autobiographical work *Not Half a Life*, without whose encouraging comments this one may never have seen the light of day. It must, however, be to my advantage that they were family and friends rather than the general reading (and paying) public.

Included in the chapter on Hong Kong are one or two minor facts lifted from *Hong Kong – Report for the Year 1967*, published by the HK Government Press, an impeccable source of impartial information on the invariable and brilliant success of government policies and actions in the colony. Hoping to jog my memory, I turned to a little guide book entitled *This is Jamaica* by a local university academic, Dr Philip Sherlock, who is quoted in the relevant chapter. I also reread George Mikes' portrait of Jamaica, *Not by Sun Alone*, which I only mention here in case I unconsciously borrowed a word or phrase. On the other hand there is no doubt at all that in my description of a short time spent in Haiti I leaned, I hope not too heavily, upon Graham Greene's excellent novel *The Comedians*.

Finally, I must once again thank my wife Helen, not only for her unfailingly kind words of encouragement, but also for her occasional forays on the internet, searching for various obscure information on my behalf. In my experience this is a time-consuming and often frustrating task. Give me a decent dictionary and a set of reference books any day.

Introduction

First things first. In case you were wondering, this book will not be a recitation of my career, which I would find difficult to reconstruct and tiresome to write about and which would risk quickly rendering you comatose. So what is it then?

I find it easier to say what it is not. It is not a travel book. It is not an attempt at a full account of the rest of my life, in the sense of a sequel to *Not Half a Life*, which came to a halt against the buffers of my twenty first birthday more than half a century ago. It is not really a sequel at all, since it is not a continuation of my story so far, though the opening chapter may briefly, and wrongly, cause you to suspect otherwise.

Let me put it like this. EC Bentley, the English writer and humorist who earned himself a small niche in literary history by inventing the comic verse form known as the 'clerihew' (his middle name which he sometimes used as pseudonym), in his *Biography for Beginners* (1905), declared that:

> *The Art of Biography*
> *Is different from Geography*
> *Geography is about Maps,*
> *But Biography is about Chaps.*

If we assume that autobiography is a sub-genre of the art in question, then what follows may be considered as either a reasonably balanced mixture of geography and biography – maps and me, if you like – or as falling fatally between the two stools, depending on your point of view.

True, my chosen title does suggest that the subject of this book is at least work-related and so, in the literal sense, it is. But I would like to reassure you. Vital as work may be to well-being and self-esteem, and despite the absurd amount of time and effort I have often invested in it, I have nonetheless always taken the view that I worked to live rather than the other way round. Broadly speaking, I share Oscar Wilde's dictum, a typically clever inversion of the original, that work is the curse of the drinking classes: like many another, there have been times when I would have preferred to be doing something else, whether drinking or not. Fortunately for me, there have been quite a lot of times when I was actually doing something else, and it usually involved getting as far away as possible from London, the calm but pressurised epicentre of the business world I inhabited for many years, preferably somewhere I could not easily be contacted by telephone.

At certain stages of my working life I spent protracted periods abroad, while at others I was based at home but made fairly frequent short visits to a wide variety of places, and for many different reasons. In these fraught times it is easy to disagree with Robert Louis Stevenson when he says 'I travel not to go anywhere, but to go. I travel for travel's sake. The great affair is to move.' That may have been fine in his more leisurely day (after all, let's not forget that his chosen means of transport was a donkey), but now, for the most part, getting from A to B is at best tedious and often a good deal worse. Though travelling itself is no pleasure at all – I dislike the whole business of flying, so much so that I have hardly boarded a plane for twenty years – the attraction for me was that it took me into new, unfamiliar environments and, equally important, gave me a real and refreshing feeling of independence from those to whom I was ultimately responsible back in London. Of course I was accountable for the decisions I made while playing away from home, so to speak, but at least they were my decisions. The work I was expected to do at my destination was sometimes interesting to me at the time and occasionally very enjoyable, but rarely could I claim that it was memorable or worthy of recounting in any great detail, so I shall try to touch only lightly upon it where it seems necessary or helpful to the narrative. My emphasis will therefore be on the places where I lived or to which I travelled rather than on the contents of the briefcase that habitually accompanied me there. Essentially I conceived this book as the story of my working life abroad, minus the work.

You will find no consistent chronological thread, though it starts at the beginning fifty years ago and drifts to a conclusion of sorts in a recent episode where the briefcase is replaced by a notional shopping bag. Apart from a certain amount of exaggeration here and understatement there, it is all more or less true. In the few instances where strict accuracy with the facts may seem to have been relaxed, it is not deliberate: in my enthusiasm I may have been carried away. At any rate, as Laurie Lee, an old favourite from my home county of Gloucestershire, put it when challenged as to the veracity of his account of his childhood in *Cider with Rosie*: 'It is the truth as I remember it. Others may remember a different truth, but that is their business.' Or words to that effect. In my experience, autobiography can range from twenty percent to eighty percent fiction. I believe what follows to be at the lower end of the spectrum.

Given that my subject here is at least partially autobiographical, I have been vaguely pondering the question of autobiography and its status in literature. Is it the refuge of the unimaginative, the easy option? The shelves of bookshops up and down the country are bulging with it. Most seems to consist of the lives of footballers or so-called celebrities, ghost-written by tabloid journalists for their idolatrous tabloid readers, so is not actually autobiography at all. Then there are the personal memoirs of professional writers, novelists and playwrights, often humorists, such as John Mortimer, Simon Gray, Clive James and even Michael Holroyd (also a serious biographer), along with countless others. These are frequently entertaining works, less because their authors have led remarkable lives than because they know how to weave a good story and do not baulk at systematic embroidery of the facts. Perhaps the extreme recent example of this is Frank McCourt, whose highly amusing autobiographical trilogy surely belongs on the fiction shelf. Add to these the poets (including Dannie Abse, Laurie Lee, and John Betjeman in verse, to name but a few), who quite properly give themselves free artistic rein, and the less imaginative, consciously scheming politicians, who recount the insider's highly partisan view of the events of their time, naturally casting themselves in a central role, and doubtless many another category of writer. All in all, then, published autobiography takes many forms and has a doubtful pedigree. Finally, there are the armies of amateurs, who research and record their and their families' histories for the benefit of children, grandchildren and unborn generations to come. Alas, they may never make it to the shelves of the local bookshop, but, good or bad, they will at least leave, as their unique bequest, something of their own creation. Something more than a few material acquisitions, sticks of furniture and the like.

Quentin Crisp in *The Naked Civil Servant* (1968) quipped that 'An autobiography is an obituary in serial form with the last instalment missing'. In this case, if indeed my book counts more as autobiography than geography, it is the last instalment.

Edging Towards A Proper Job

The tendency to defer to another day any decision on a career came naturally to me. It wasn't so much that I was lazy, though I undoubtedly was; rather that I didn't have the first idea what I wanted to do with my life. But that is putting it far too grandly. Having no sense of vocation nor even any conscious preference for a particular type of occupation, I found it difficult if not impossible to take the long view. Besides, I had only the foggiest notion of what might be involved in the world of work in commerce and industry (perish the thought) and as for the professions, they sounded more interesting but unfortunately required qualifications that I neither possessed nor saw myself acquiring. A role in the public sector never crossed my mind. The one thing I had on my side was time, plenty of it, so I could afford a bit of procrastination.

I had just emerged into the competitive rough and tumble of civilian life from the relative security of national service in the Army. So, despite the cushion of nearly £100 in the bank, my immediate priority was to find myself a job to pay my day-to-day living expenses, including the £3 per week rent on my shared flat in West Hampstead, NW6 – a decent enough address if lacking the cachet of Hampstead, NW3. The obvious answer was to take temporary employment, of which there was no shortage, while I carefully considered my longer term future. With the Christmas shopping madness looming I was happy to be taken on by the Oxford Street department store Selfridges for seasonal work as a shop assistant, one of many young people with my sort of background and in my sort of predicament, at a loose end and in need of cash. Placed initially in Wines and Spirits, I was soon moved to Liqueur Chocolates and thence to Men's Shoes, which seemed to me a rapid descent to about as low as I could go. But it had its advantages. Those of my friends who were kicking their heels without gainful employment would come in for a chat, trying on numerous pairs of shoes they had no intention of buying until it was time to escape to the pub across the road in Duke Street. A steady income of £9 per week made it easy to put off for a while any serious ambitions of a career, so when my spell at Selfridges reached its natural and welcome conclusion following the new year sales I quickly slipped into another job with no apparent prospects, although technically I was taken on as a permanent member of staff.

This time it was a menial position, labelled trainee, in a miserable little company that sold advertising space, or placed advertisements in newspapers or did something I never really understood which was in some way related to advertising, though it had no creative role in the process. If asked what I did for a living, especially if it was an attractive girl doing the asking, I would say vaguely that I was in advertising, thus hinting at the glamorous world of filming, copywriting or account management, whatever that might be. I became adept at deflecting further lines of enquiry which might have revealed the pathetic truth of the matter. If I had ever dreamed that this appointment might present me with an opening into the real world of advertising (unintended oxymoron), that notion was soon abandoned. So too was the job, which I managed to escape before being sucked down into the state of chronic clinical depression that seemed to afflict the few other employees, whose generous conditions of employment allowed them to flee their Dickensian premises for a full half an hour at lunchtime and two weeks' paid holiday a year.

And so it continued, this drift from one dead-end job to the next, although I should stress that outside working hours life was fun – too much fun to allow time for thinking about the serious business of a career. There was the lowly clerical function at the Bank of England, where a friend and I performed the mind-numbing task of checking through endless piles of old cheques, though to what purpose I have not the slightest recollection, if indeed I ever knew. I do remember that the process was referred to in the Bank as 'looking back'. We decided a better term for the whole ridiculous business was 'looking backwards' and we had very soon done enough of that, thank you. We were more interested in looking forwards.

Working for a while in a pub was passable and could even be fun if friends were visiting, but it was poorly paid and I didn't much like the unsocial hours, that is to say working when others were enjoying themselves within view. At least my departure was conventional, unlike that of another friend who, irritated beyond measure by the nagging demands of his boss the land-lord, tendered his instant resignation, literally vaulted the bar and spent the rest of the evening drinking with his friends and erstwhile customers, insisting on taking in kind the wages he was owed for that evening's work.

At some point in this sequence of casual occupations I spotted an advertisement in the Evening Standard for a job as a salesman in the City. Ah, the City. Despite my brief and excruciating experience at the Old Lady of Threadneedle Street, mention of the City still conjured up images of serious respectability, the deal sealed with a handshake, one's word is one's bond, and so on. I applied and was invited for interview. Perhaps this would turn out to be a proper job, the start of something decent, a job I could openly admit to doing.

Then again, perhaps not. I was interviewed – I use the term in its loosest sense – by the Managing Director and the Sales Director. The MD was a reserved, sombrely dressed, middle-aged man, apparently lacking in self-confidence, apt to break into a nervous chuckle, with a round face, a florid complexion, strong east London accent and a slightly incongruous Homburg, without which, as I came to know, he never set foot outside. His colleague was a bit younger, about forty-five, Essex born and bred I would guess, an irrepressible extrovert character with more than a touch of flashiness about him, his invariable brown trilby at a rakish angle. In short, they were both very agreeable. They were evidently impressed with my modest CV, which told them little more than that I had attended a school they had never heard of, passed my A Levels and held a commission in the Army. From this they deduced that I was an educated chap, a gent, and they were thus more than happy for me to interview them about their company, just occasionally dropping hints to the effect that I might find it a trifle mundane after my exotic experiences elsewhere.

The company was in stationery, manufacturing specialised rolls of paper for use in teleprinters and the like, which it sold direct to firms located mainly in the City and points east, many of which in those pre-computer days had serried ranks of such machines operating round the clock. It occupied premises in Curtain Road, a rather grubby back street somewhere in the dark hinterland behind Liverpool Street station. Physically it was not far from the square mile; in every other sense it was a million miles away. Apart from the two directors, the staff consisted of a factory supervisor and three or four female machine operators in headscarves; an office manager responsible for the accounts, billing, inventory control and everything clerical, who had spent his whole adult life there and who consequently knew all there was to know about suppliers, customers and the internal workings of the company; and finally a kind of secretary and general dogsbody who did the typing and everything that fell between the cracks.

Despite all this, and much to their surprise, I agreed to join them as a salesman. No, as *the* salesman, the only member of the sales staff other than the director. Without me he would have had nobody to direct, not that he did much of that, as we shall see. I justified this decision to myself on the grounds that sales experience of any kind in the City would be a useful addition to my CV and that I would be rubbing shoulders with influential City types, so who could say what further opportunities might present themselves? My acceptance of the post was gratefully received, on the sole condition that I wore, or at least owned, a hat, type unspecified. That being settled, we repaired to the pub over the road to start getting the feel of things.

It took me no time at all to realise that I was totally unsuited to the job. I seemed to possess none of the qualities required of a successful salesman. I could barely bring myself to attempt to persuade buyers of the superiority of our possibly inferior products (actually I could see no difference between ours and anybody else's); I lacked the skill, or the will, to overcome objections (an essential attribute of the salesman), recognising too readily that these objections were perfectly rational; I was far too thin-skinned and showed insufficient perseverance. Leaving aside my own deficiencies as a salesman, however, the real problem lay with the buyers, my potential customers. It was most unfair: they weren't at all what I had expected. Far from being City gents they were invariably raw, rough-edged East End types who shot from the hip and had no time for pleasantries with some namby-pamby sales tyro.

If I rang first for an appointment I found it difficult to get through to the buyer, more often than not being given the brush-off by some Eliza Doolittle of a junior secretary, for whom rejecting a well-spoken salesman was doubtless the highlight of her day and who probably didn't even bother to consult her boss on the subject. Since I was obliged to make these calls from the general office, my failures were rather public and all the more painful for that, so I decided that cold calling might be less embarrassing and perhaps more effective. But no, cold calling was an absolute nightmare. The chances were that the buyer wouldn't see me. When he agreed to do so, he would probably keep me waiting for so long that by the time he confronted me, for that was how it felt, I was a gibbering wreck. Why should he buy from me when he already had a most dependable, satisfactory supplier? Sorry, who were we again? – he'd mislaid my business card which had been passed to him, what, just half an hour earlier. Never heard of you, you new in the business? The quality's too low and the price too high. You need to get the price right down. The arguments seemed to me insuperable. What was I to do?

Well, that was the one question to which I had a ready answer: I would stop calling. That is to say, I would stop trying to sell anything. In short, I would stop working. Then it would simply be a matter of time before my de facto withdrawal of labour became apparent to my employers and they took the only appropriate action. In the meantime I could still claim to have a job and my monthly salary, however unearned and undeserved, would continue to be slipped quietly into my bank account.

I fell into the habit of rising late and dressing as if for work. Usually I would then meet friends for a couple of pints followed by lunch, either at the pub or at a City restaurant such as George and the Dragon, where a substantial meal could be had for 2/6d, making dinner redundant. Occasionally, maybe once a week, I would creep into the office, expecting fire and brimstone to descend on my head, only to be greeted with a cheery welcome and otherwise largely ignored. Often Mr Carrington, the office factotum, would pass me some mail which might contain one or two small orders from existing customers, on which he would congratulate me in his deadpan way. I was quite sure he knew full well that those orders were routine and would have arrived anyway, even if I had not existed, which to all intents and purposes I did not. Learning of my presence in the office the MD Mr Parker – nobody here appeared to have been blessed with a first name – would put his head round the door to enquire if I 'would care to take a small libation with me, Mr Knight'. Before long he would don his hat for the fifty yard walk and off we would go to the pub, to be joined shortly by Mr Weatherhead the Sales Director, the timing of whose arrival could only have been achieved by telepathic communication with Mr P, as he called the MD when he was in a bouncy mood, which to be fair was most of the time. Having regaled us with tales of his latest brilliantly marshalled sales campaign, or perhaps laid into some obstinately uncooperative prospect, Mr W would invariably signal the end of business talk by launching into a round of new jokes, most of which were fit only for the ears of the men who populated the saloon bar. At this point I could breathe a sigh of relief that my own activities, or rather the lack of them, were once again to escape the probing scrutiny of my senior management. In fact the nearest they ever came to it was for one or other to ask 'Everything alright then, Mr Knight?', while not bothering to wait for an answer.

This pattern was repeated week after week, month after month. Sometimes Mr Weatherhead might say 'Here's a lead, Mr Knight. When you have a moment, why not drop in and see this chap? I think we might be lucky here.' I loved that 'when you have a moment'. So I would call as requested and, if we were indeed lucky, would come away with a small trial order in my pocket, Mr W having previously done all the hard work of softening up the prospect. As time passed, however, and nothing changed, I felt increasingly uncomfortable. In the face of all the evidence to date I nonetheless feared I might at any minute be summoned for a performance review and my monstrous deceit would be laid bare. As I say, there was nothing to suggest this might happen, given the fact that my occasional sales report, entirely fabricated as it was, had never been questioned and no business meeting of any sort had ever taken place outside of the saloon bar. It had even crossed my mind that this might have something to do with class deference:

that my bosses might simply have been reluctant to challenge someone of officer class and preferred to let events take their course.

Which of course they did. My feelings of guilt at doing nothing to earn the salary I was paid grew steadily to the point at which I could no longer live with them. I submitted my resignation and it was accepted with apparent surprise and disappointment, though this was almost certainly feigned since Mr P remarked that, frankly, he always knew I was destined for better things. On our final visit to the pub I was fêted as if I had been the company's star performer and I was not allowed to pay for any drinks. Such was the atmosphere of celebration that Mr Weatherhead, in saying farewell, momentarily forgot himself and addressed me for the first and only time by my Christian name.

Before turning my back on my friends at the paper supplies firm I had in fact taken the precaution of securing another position, this time in a large, reputable high technology company which would provide me with a sound business and technical sales training. It happened like this.

Though not myself a graduate, and by inclination and education anything but technical, I nonetheless applied for a place on a graduate trainee scheme with an international computer company, with a view to subsequent appointment as a Technical Advisor. Given my obvious shortcomings I was more than a little surprised to be invited for an interview. It took place in a plush office in Mayfair and was conducted by the company's Personnel Director, a fellow with something of a military bearing who went by the aristocratic sounding name of Seymour Dearden. He could not have been more different from my then current employers. His eye was caught by two features of my CV upon which the whole interview was to be concentrated. The first was my national service commission in the so-called Glorious Gloucesters and my secondment to Sierra Leone, an experience he seemed to take as proof of my enquiring mind and adventurous spirit. The second was the fact that I played rugby, which he clearly regarded as character-forming in a way that, say, three years at a good university was not. The two and a half years that I had just spent messing about getting nowhere was never raised; the Army and rugby obviously trumped any possible negatives.

Having been sufficiently impressed with these desirable personal qualities of mine, Mr (Colonel? General?) Dearden stood up and was on the point of shaking hands, telling me that I would receive confirmation of my appointment in the post within days, when I suddenly hit on what turned out to be a brilliant idea. To understand a little more of what my potential role as a Technical Advisor would involve, I wondered if it might be possible, before finalising my decision, to meet someone who was actually doing the job. I was rather pleased with the unspoken way I had hinted at other irons in the fire. Seymour Dearden resumed his seat. Had I scored a good point or had I slightly irritated him with my unexpected request? Whichever it was, he quickly recovered to say, 'Why, of course, an excellent suggestion', whereupon he picked up the telephone and dialled. 'Good morning, James. Seymour Dearden here. I've got a young chap with me, thinking of joining the company, would like to have a chat with a TA. Could you spare an hour or so one day next week? A spot of lunch perhaps? Name's Peter Knight. Jolly good. Your office, midday on Tuesday then. Thanks.'

A few days later when I arrived at the company's West

End office as arranged, I discovered that I was not alone in having requested a meeting with a so-called TA. Noel Chandler was a couple of years older than me but our recent backgrounds were not entirely dissimilar. After two years at Bristol University Noel had tired of reading law, left and spent his national service as a subaltern with the Jamaica Regiment. He was also a rugby player. James Johnson turned out to be younger than both of us, a pleasant and easy-going Old Etonian who I suspect may have moved in the same social circles as Seymour Dearden. Without any preliminaries he suggested lunch at his club, a short walk away in Berkeley Square, and we were soon ensconced in deep leather armchairs with large gin and tonics – a situation thoroughly familiar to Noel and me from our days in the mess. In due course, unhurriedly, we proceeded to an agreeable lunch with a couple of bottles of decent claret, followed by large cognacs and modest cigars. I recall no discussion of the company or the role of a Technical Advisor, but we had seen enough to gain a generally favourable impression of the company ethos.

At about two-thirty James said he hoped we would excuse him: he should be getting back to the office, where he had a busy afternoon ahead of him. We were less than convinced of this, reckoning that James was sufficiently under the weather to justify an early return home, having in any case spent a satisfactory day netting two recruits to the fold. So we thanked him and said our goodbyes on the steps of his club, letting him get well away before we moved off, not wishing to cause him embarrassment at being seen to turn in the opposite direction from the office. With just time for a pint before afternoon closing, Noel and I strolled north out of Berkeley Square. Within a few yards we were both struck by the same thought, simultaneously expressed: on the evidence available, this seemed to be our sort of company.

And so it proved, at least in those early days, despite the fact that we were miserably paid. Admittedly during our training period we benefited from free board and lodging, which meant that our earnings were effectively beer money, but the whole working environment was quite different from today, as were the attitudes of some paternalistic managers who couldn't see the way the wind was blowing. Around that time the toff Seymour Dearden was approached by a fully-trained graduate Technical Advisor complaining of the difficulty of making ends meet on his meagre salary.

'I need an immediate rise,' he said, 'because I am not being paid enough to live on. If you can't agree to an increase of £500 minimum I shall have to look elsewhere for a job that pays a living wage. I'm sure you will accept that this would be unfortunate, given that the company has just invested so much in my training.'

The logic of his argument seemed to be lost on the Personnel Director whose response was merely to enquire, 'Can't your father help you?' At about the same time a well qualified friend of mine was working for peanuts at one of the famous London art auction houses. He also appealed for an increase, to which the reply was even less sympathetic: 'If you can't afford to work here, you will just have to look elsewhere.' Which he did without further ado.

Assam Is More Than Just Tea

In the mid-sixties I got mixed up in oil. It started at Shell-Mex and BP, the retail company jointly owned by the two giant oil producers and set up to market their products in the United Kingdom.

The Head Office was a splendid building on the Strand, a few paces from the Savoy Hotel. I was sent there to program the computer we had just sold them and with a vague remit to train some of their staff, in order that they could continue the work when I had moved on. The second of those tasks was casually brushed aside, since the staff concerned had no intention of making fools of themselves with the new technology and their manager seemed not to bother one way or the other. My potential 'trainees' were all about twice my age and quite content to cruise through the remaining years of their working lives doing what they had always done, which was designing accounting systems. Although they shied away from practical involvement in my activity, they did me the courtesy of following my progress with some curiosity and above all they were very friendly. They looked up to me as some sort of technical genius, which made me wonder how they might have reacted to a real one, the sort we kept hidden from customers who might otherwise have tempted them away with much gold. They would invite me to join them for lunch in the company dining room (it was far too grand to be called a canteen) at the heavily subsidised price of 1/3d (6p) for three courses and coffee.

Working in such an environment was most agreeable, if not especially challenging, but I was soon required elsewhere.

Having acquitted myself well at Shell-Mex I was assigned to other customers for short periods of technical assistance, where I demonstrated the truth of the old maxim that in the land of the blind the one-eyed man is king. One deployment was to the frozen foods company MacFisheries at Bracknell, which was then a pretty village with a lovely and well-used rural pub and is now a hideous agglomeration of office buildings and vast multi-storey car parks, disfiguring the once beautiful Berkshire countryside. Somewhere amongst all this there is presumably a town, a residential area with the usual amenities, but I have never managed to find it.

Another assignment was to an aeronautics factory in Oldham, the least attractive town I can ever recall visiting if you ignore Lagos, though its Lancastrian inhabitants were infinitely more agreeable than those of the Nigerian capital, as I was to discover nearly a decade later. There I stayed in the attic of a gloomy terraced house offering bed, breakfast and dinner for 17/6d (87.5p) a day, plus an extra 6d for a bath, to which my accommodation allowance could just about be made to stretch. My hostess would be quite perplexed and took it almost as a personal affront if I declined a second helping of hotpot or steak and kidney pudding at dinner. She seemed to see it as part of her job to build me up to be fit for hard physical work, treating me as if I spent my days as a navvy, digging roads rather than sitting at a desk programming a computer.

My only previous experience of the north of England was a spell of about three months working in Sheffield. Several of our customers were in the steel industry, which dominated the city in those days. They were all located in the district of Brightside, named with heavy irony as it was permanently overhung with such a dense pall of smoke from the factories that neither sky nor sun was ever visible from the ground. On my arrival by train I made for the nearest pub and ordered a pint, in a mug as I've always preferred it.

'Glass of bitter, luv?' said the bored barmaid and brought me a half.

'Sorry, I asked for a pint.'

'Oh, I thought you said a glass.' She gave me a look of incomprehension and returned to the pump to pull me a pint in a straight glass. I thought a second might be tempting fate, so I caught a bus to my digs and the burly unshaven conductor wound me out a ticket.

'That'll be fourpence, luv.'

'Thanks. Could you let me know when we reach my stop, please?'

'My pleasure, luv.'

I hadn't been there five minutes but I was beginning to wonder about the people of Sheffield and to feel like a foreigner in what I thought was my own land.

For the duration of my stay I rented a modest bedsitter with small kitchen and bathroom and, most importantly, its own separate entrance, which I felt gave me a degree of independence and privacy. My landlady had other ideas. After a while I met a girl, a southerner like me and also new to the strange customs of the north. She was a trainee journalist working on the Sheffield Telegraph, one of the highly regarded provincial dailies which I think belonged to the Thomson Group of newspapers. One evening we were heading for my place. We had barely put a foot on the first of the steps leading up to my door when the landlady appeared on her porch. I wished her a cheery 'Good night', but instead of responding in kind she said:

'There'll be no females in your room, Mr Knight. Not now nor any other time. This is not London, you know.'

Well, I thought, you can say that again. She must have passed her evenings hovering behind the net curtains waiting for the return of her wicked tenant. I made a mental note to send a small donation to the Yorkshire Independence Party.

Perhaps to build on my experience of the petroleum industry I was despatched to Hampshire for a few weeks to do a job at the Esso Oil refinery at Fawley, about which I remember nothing except that, just as at Shell-Mex, the staff facilities were brilliant. No doubt this reflected the paternalistic culture of the business (once in, employees were so well looked after that they never wanted to leave), as well as the need to defray some small part of the enormous profits they routinely recorded. At any rate the oil companies seemed also to be in catering in a big way.

At about the same time I was given my first full responsibility for a customer account, the Iraq Petroleum Company (IPC), whose headquarters overlooked Oxford Circus. If this sounds rather grand, it was in reality a sinecure. IPC was not a sales opportunity, neither did they need any technical support, being destined for extinction as a separate company in the near future. I hit it off very well with the data processing manager who was approaching retirement after a career spent largely in Iraq. His name was Ted Norman and I called him Lord Ted, rather as Dexter the England cricket captain, who wasn't a Lord either. Roughly once a month he and I would meet for a liquid lunch at The Cock in Great Portland Street, where business was not permitted to sully the conversation. Afterwards he would ask if I would care to 'visit the shop' and, with a chuckle, before I could reply he would add something like 'No, I agree, there's not much point in that. Well, give me a ring, Peter, when you feel like popping over.' Whereupon I would head for Tottenham Court Road and the Northern Line back home to Hampstead.

Of course I did have other things on my plate. British Petroleum's investment in our computer systems ran to several millions of pounds, making it one of the company's largest commercial accounts. There were major installations at Head Office and in the three UK refineries in Scotland, Wales and Kent. We had a substantial team dedicated to the profitable development of the BP account, led by a senior man with the ear of top management and including several sales and technical staff. Presumably on the theory that I had by now gained considerable practical experience of the oil industry, I was given charge of our business with the refinery at Llandarcy, near Neath in South Wales. If so, the theory was wrong. True, I had become vaguely familiar with a few particular concepts such as LP, which stood for Linear Programming and referred to an enormously powerful mathematical model that BP (and no doubt all the others) used as its primary strategic tool to optimise its worldwide logistical operations. I also knew that catalytic crackers had nothing to do with Christmas but performed some sort of chemical separation and could be easily identified as the chimneys that belched flames in any refinery. Those on the inside called them cat crackers. It is on such wafer-thin knowledge that one can pose as a specialist, or be mistaken for an expert.

My introduction to BP Llandarcy was not the most auspicious. I was due to meet their senior management team over a buffet lunch after delivering a talk on computers in general and the role of their computer in the running of the refinery. Two days before this appointment I acquired my first wholly owned motor car (I had previously enjoyed a half share in one), a utilitarian, unlovely Vauxhall, bought second hand from a friend at the rugby club. Having decided to drive down to Llandarcy, I booked a hotel in Neath so that I should be on the spot and fresh for the meeting the following morning. Unfortunately things didn't work out quite as planned. I was within a couple of miles of my hotel when, in darkness and driving rain I must have suffered a temporary lapse of concentration and I skidded into the back of a lorry which, in my dazed recollection, braked sharply without warning, having suddenly decided to turn right. The collision jolted me forward and my head struck the rear mirror with sufficient force to cause quite a deep cut. I may have been bleeding profusely, but my car was mortally wounded. An ambulance took me to Neath General Hospital, where I was stitched up and admitted, or rather detained for observation overnight, something that was standard practice in the case of head injuries. Naturally I was in no fit state to fulfil my commitments on the following day. Instead I was put on a train back to London, with messages of sympathy and, in all probability, sighs of relief that my intended audience had been spared the tedium of a lecture on computing by some bright-eyed, bushy-tailed young upstart.

Over the next year or two I was a frequent visitor to Llandarcy, where I was always given a warm Welsh welcome. I developed a strong relationship with my chief contact, the computer manager. In fact our relationship was positively conspiratorial. He was a short, dapper man, always immaculately turned out and good-humoured. But this affability tended to disguise a hard edge, a scheming personality, which is not unknown in people with real ambition. He had plenty of this but it was rather narrowly focused. He wasn't interested, for example, in a move to a bigger job in London. Nor did he seek promotion locally, except in the sense of a better title, which he later achieved: director rather than manager. What he craved was to be recognised as a trail blazer, to be seen as the leading light in computing in the refineries. For that he had to create at Llandarcy a computer system that was bigger and better than those run by his colleagues at Grangemouth in Scotland and the Isle of Grain in Kent, whom he saw first as competitors, later as subordinates. We seemed to spend all our time planning, or plotting, the expansion of his empire. All of which benefited me greatly as the orders flowed in. He was doing my work for me.

Then out of the blue came a request from our international division: our Indian company thought they had a good prospect for a computer sale, but lacked the expertise to carry out the necessary study and make an appropriate recommendation. They needed the help of a specialist in the petroleum industry, who, to my initial consternation, turned out to be me. Well, the assignment was good news insofar as it would take me to an interesting part of the world, but it also brought the alarming possibility that I might be exposed as a charlatan, whose knowledge of the industry was at best superficial and who was grossly underqualified for the technical challenge involved in refinery systems analysis and design. I seriously considered declining the invitation, for it was more in the nature of a request than a command, but eventually decided to take the risk. My decision was also influenced by the fact that the company would pay for a lightweight suit and other clothes for the tropics and, with more or less everything found, it would be an opportunity to save some of my paltry salary.

I arrived in Bombay (as it still was, before being renamed Mumbai) in early September. The heat and humidity were such that in the few yards between the transfer bus and the terminal my smart new suit lost all shape and dripped as if I had been caught in a tropical downpour. Our sales director for India, an Englishman who had spent his whole career on the subcontinent, was there to greet me.

'Welcome to India, Peter. Your first time?' He shook my hand warmly.

'Yes. I come in all innocence' I replied.

'I think you'll enjoy it.' he said. 'Do you like cricket?'

'Like it? No, I'm fanatical.'

'That's even better. I've got tickets for the test match tomorrow. I haven't arranged anything for this evening as I felt you might prefer to settle in and get a decent night's sleep after the journey. If that's OK, I'll drop you at your hotel and pick you up in the morning at about ten o'clock.'

'Terrific. Thank you very much.' I was quite happy to have the evening to myself, since I guessed it might be the last for a while.

We drove to the old Brabourne Stadium the following morning and I'm sure I thought nothing of the ease with which we entered the ground and parked in a most convenient spot. It was only later that I discovered that Jack had for many years played Ranji Trophy cricket for Bombay, having been a first class wicket-keeper, and was therefore a much respected local character. West Indies was the touring side, but I remember very little about the play that day, the result of the match or the outcome of the series. Three images remain in my mind: first the rare, even unique, sight of Wes Hall, one of the all-time great fast bowlers, being elegantly stroked straight back over his head to the boundary by the slight figure of the Nawab of Pataudi, lately of Winchester, Oxford and Sussex, now captain of India, whose very presence on the cricket field was something of a miracle as he had lost the sight in his right eye in a car accident a few years earlier; secondly, the celebratory fire-crackers with which this shot and others were greeted all over the ground; and finally the fires that were started in the cheap wooden stands every time misfortune struck and India lost a wicket. The risk of consequences far more catastrophic than a setback in the game seemed to bother neither the crowd nor the security services, if indeed any such body existed.

The timing of my arrival in Bombay was even luckier than I could have imagined. The following day was a rest day in this match so that evening there was a party in the pavilion to which Jack had been invited and I went as his guest. There I met all the players of both sides, plus those who were on tour but not selected for this test, including the nineteen year old Clive Lloyd, on his first tour but destined to become an outstanding captain of West Indies before very long. Gathered in that room were some of the foremost cricketers of the 1960s and 1970s and I was fortunate enough to find myself in conversation with many of them. The very idea of such a party in the middle of a test match, with the two teams socialising as if it was the most natural thing in the world, would be inconceivable in the hard-bitten professional game today.

Bombay was not my ultimate destination, nor was New Delhi but that was where I went next. Word had been passed round that I was visiting the country, so all our local managers were hoping to profit from my presence by taking me to see customers with whom they were having difficulties or by seeking my help to clinch a sale. Whatever the situation it was assumed that I would have the answer, that I would be able to achieve in no time at all what they had been struggling to do for months or even years. After all, I was the expert from Head Office. Oh dear, how I must have disappointed them. I sprinkled my magic to no effect and moved on to Calcutta.

I was impressed with our people in this seething ant-hill of a city. Several of them were considerably more experienced than I was, with better qualifications in both the sales and technical fields. It struck me as very odd, and not a little extravagant, that I had been brought all the way from London to do a job that I was quite sure any one of half a dozen local staff could have done at least equally well and probably better. In the end I suppose it was just a matter of confidence: they lacked it and I was automatically assumed to have it, particularly when dealing with Europeans, as I was going to do.

Allow me a tiny diversion here to recount a story from the world of music which seems to me, in a funny sort of way, apposite to my situation. In Paris the renowned Romanian violinist and composer George Enescu agreed, no doubt for compelling financial reasons, to give violin lessons to the son of his bank manager, a boy of no obvious musical talent or potential. After some time and modest progress the bank manager suggested that his son was surely ready to play a recital. He would organise it and take care of the costs if Enescu would look after the musical side of things. Generously, though presumably in an effort to reduce the risk of disaster, the Romanian master proposed that he himself should provide the piano accompaniment. Arrangements were duly made and shortly before the date of the recital Enescu mentioned it rather forlornly to his friend Alfred Cortot, the great French pianist, who immediately volunteered to come along and turn the pages. The invited audience included a couple of music critics known to the bank manager, one of whom later summed up the event succinctly: the page turner should have been playing the piano, the pianist should have been playing the violin and the violinist should have been turning the pages.

Without wishing to stretch a point too far, I felt I was being asked to play the violin when maybe I was better suited to the job of page turner.

Anyway, for two or three days they shuttled me round town in their rickety old cars through the chaotic Calcutta traffic, each journey a hair-raising adventure and a miraculous demonstration of the art of survival against all the odds. In those streets pedestrians, bicycles, rickshaws, private cars, taxis, buses and lorries, not to mention the various animals, all competed for the same space, with apparently no agreed rules of engagement. Everybody drove with one hand on the wheel and the other on the horn, so the noise was continuous and deafening. The quality of the air was off the bottom of any conceivable scale: a soup-like concoction of exhaust fumes, the stale smell of old cooking and the stench of rotting litter. Added to which was the sheer numbers of people on the street. Was India the origin of the word mayhem?

They took me to a hot prospect where they felt that 'just one more heave' would get that elusive signature on a contract, but obviously the company concerned was playing a longer game. I was put in to bat, sparkled briefly but couldn't deliver. An existing customer was unhappy. He had problems of reliability of his equipment: what could I do? Well, I could offer a smile and a few soothing words, even a promise to refer the matter up to some mythical higher authority with which I was closely in touch. But as for actually doing anything, there was no chance. I wasn't an engineer and had no idea what went on under the bonnet. We paid a visit to a utilities company whose computer had been rendered ineffective by a walkout of the operations staff. They hadn't walked far: no further than the pavement directly outside the main entrance to the building in which the system was housed. There they took up traditional squatting positions, their legs crossed in the manner of Mahatma Gandhi or as I always imagined fakirs on a bed of nails, in a solidly impassable picket, not that any of their trades union comrades were attempting to cross the line. It was unclear exactly what their principal grievance was, but amongst other things they were demanding that additional staff should be recruited. Their position appeared to be that if their employer could afford to install a computer, then they could afford to take on a few of Calcutta's tens of thousands of unemployed. In the meantime the shiny new computer had been sitting there for several months, having only ever been switched on for the official inauguration ceremony, from which no doubt the lowly operators would have been excluded anyway. I'm not quite sure whether my role on this occasion was to show solidarity with the management or with the strikers. I failed to see how any attitude I might adopt could do other than inflame a situation that seemed for the time being calm enough, with both sides waiting for the other to blink first. In India you could literally believe the cliché that 'time stood still'.

While I was in Calcutta trying to boost the morale of my Indian colleagues by these various interventions, however obviously fatuous, I stayed at a fantastic hotel called The Grand. The picture I retain is of large public rooms, wood-panelled or with papered walls either peeling or threatening imminently to do so, strewn with a charmingly random selection of armchairs, settees and occasional tables, clubby and comfortable but in the strictest sense past their best. The few scattered rugs left uncovered acres of dark floorboards with the beautiful patina of age, the passage of countless feet and the almost incessant polishing by generations of dedicated hotel servants. The dining rooms were equally vast, their tables a mixture of square, rectangular and round all spread with an incalculable area of brilliant white linen. But the overwhelming impression was of fans, scores perhaps hundreds of gleaming brass or elegant wooden blades circling endlessly above you wherever you chose to stand, sit or lounge. They circled rather than whirled, turning just fast enough to stir the air but not with sufficient energy to cause a perceptible down-draught. Their effect was not so much to cool the space beneath them as to give the feeling that there was more fresh air than was actually the case. However many people thronged the sitting rooms and however hot the temperature outside, the atmosphere never became unbearably stuffy and to my mind was infinitely superior to that produced by air conditioning, which sucks out the humidity and can leave you with a sore throat and a nasty chill.

There was not much grass to be seen anywhere else in Calcutta, but if you were lucky enough to be a guest at the Grand Hotel you couldn't miss it. Leaving the hotel you had only to pick your way through the throng of parked taxis and rickshaws, whose eager drivers clamoured for your custom at any hour of day or night, and, perhaps taking your life in your hands, cross Jawaharlal Nehru Road. There, spread out for as far as the eye could see, was the *maidan*, a long flat grassy strip on which the citizens of Calcutta could take their leisure, strolling, picnicking or playing games. At certain times you could only do the latter and then only if you were a member of a team. I went for a walk along the edge of the *maidan* when there must have been a dozen or more cricket matches taking place, all side by side, for the depth of the strip could accommodate no more than a single game at any point. There was no space between them and it may well be that the playing areas overlapped, with the potential for great confusion as to who was playing in which match and which ball belonged to whom. Yet I imagine these were club games of a sort, because they seemed to be being played in all seriousness. My mind went back to this scene when, years later and in an entirely different context, I walked on Ipanema Beach in Rio de Janeiro and saw serious club football matches being played, surrounded by large numbers of partisan spectators, the pitches laid out similarly in single file the whole way along the sand.

Before going to India I had never heard of the Fokker Friendship, the Brahmaputra or Dibrugarh. When

I left Calcutta I did so by boarding the first, which followed the second and finally landed at the third. The Fokker Friendship was a small commercial aircraft with a capacity, from memory, of about twenty or so passengers. In common with other Indian internal airlines, this one carried a lot more than passengers, notably the entire contents of their homes including various livestock. You could find yourself seated next to a small goat and sundry raucous chickens. I wasn't very keen on this aeroplane and even less so when it appeared that the chief navigational aids were rivers, while we lacked the capability to land on water.

The airport that serves Calcutta is called Dum Dum, which is vaguely disconcerting for a start. We set off in a north easterly direction and seemed to trace a path along a network of minor rivers, tributaries of something or other, until we reached a big one. This turned out to be the Brahmaputra, which at that point runs due south through Bangladesh, a country not yet invented in the mid-1960s when it was still known as East Pakistan, eventually to join forces with the Ganges, the sacred river of the Hindus, and empty itself into the Bay of Bengal. The Brahmaputra is an amazing river. It rises in the Himalayas in China, somewhere to the north of Nepal, where it's called something different, flows more or less due east for a few hundred miles before turning south across the little-known, or in my case unknown, Arunachal Pradesh, the most extreme north-easterly state of India. On reaching Assam it does another sharp right turn and proceeds to bisect that state for its full length until, at its western border, it heads south for the sea. The river is 1800 miles long, making it longer if not greater than the Ganges.

We followed the river north at low altitude so as

not to get lost in the clouds, turned right at the border and landed first at Gauhati, which is probably the capital of Assam because it boasts an International Airport. From there the Fokker Friendship, still in close alliance with the Brahmaputra, took us to Dibrugarh, possibly by way of Tezpur and Jorhat, though after so many years I can't be sure of that. At Dibrugarh I was met by a welcoming Scot, probably pleased to see a new face, who drove me on the last leg of my long journey from Hampstead, London to the small town of Digboi, Upper Assam, where the Assam Oil Company had (and has) oil production facilities and a refinery in which I was to have the pleasure of spending the next nine or ten weeks.

Oil was first discovered in the area in the 1880s. Engineers working on the extension of a railway line to the nearby town of Ledo were using elephants for haulage of timber for the track. Legend has it that they noticed an oily substance on the legs of the elephants as they emerged from the forest at a certain point. They tracked back and found a spot where oil was seeping from the ground. So far the story is perfectly credible. One of the engineers, an Englishman, is then said to have urged a worker to 'Dig, boy', a cry which was subsequently adopted as the name of the place of discovery. Since oil was initially struck at a depth of 178 feet, that would have been some dig. Indeed, that would have been some boy.

From Digboi you can't go far in any direction except south-west without finding yourself in an unfriendly foreign country or a potentially dangerous territory. Sweeping round in an arc from the west to the north-west there is the mountainous and virtually uninhabited Indian state of Arunachal Pradesh as a buffer between Assam and China. But it's very confusing because when

I was in Digboi this state didn't exist: it was then something called the North East Frontier Agency of Assam. To the east there is Burma and to the south Nagaland, which is an Indian state but reluctantly so, having been agitating for some form of independence for as long as anyone can remember. Apparently the Nagas are a warlike tribe of hunter gatherers but I'm not in a position to confirm that hearsay since, not wishing to be hunted or gathered, I stayed clear of them.

The people at Assam Oil, on the other hand, could not have been more generous. For a start they gave me a bungalow overlooking the golf course and just a few minutes' stroll up the gentle slope leading from my place of work. What is more, they lent me a set of clubs and the freedom of the course was mine, though it might not have been if they had witnessed my early efforts at hacking a ball round. They invited me to their houses and to any parties that were going. There I also met educated Indians who sounded as if they came from a background of Harrow and Oxbridge, but who it transpired had never actually left India and possibly had not crossed the borders of Assam.

Upper Assam is a beautiful part of the world. Hilly but not mountainous, despite the proximity of the Himalayas, it spreads out on either side of the shallow valley through which the Brahmaputra rolls seawards, albeit with a long way yet to go, and its landscapes are wonderfully varied. It encompasses dense, wild jungle such as we associate with the northern part of Burma, which after all is a near neighbour, and cultivated land exemplified by, though not limited to, the vast yet orderly tea plantations that, viewed from a high vantage point, often stretch as far as the eye can see. Assam is a very rural state, growing a variety of crops in the communal plots around the many small towns and villages.

Oil refineries are usually ugly, dirty and smelly places, or at least they used to be. Advances in technology have doubtless cleaned things up somewhat, but if so the improvements would not yet have arrived when I was at Digboi. Even so, my recollection is that the refinery somehow managed not to cast its industrial shadow too darkly over the surrounding countryside. As I walked down to my office in the cool early morning sunshine I would look across a dreamy landscape lightly shrouded in a fine white mist. This would shortly be burned off to reveal a scene of multi-coloured vegetation in which the local people went about their daily work, often accompanied by their animals, whose tinkling bells created a faintly alpine air. The days were hot, but by no means unbearably so, and typically ended with a spectacular sunset, the whole tableau bathed in a rich red glow before nightfall brought its abrupt extinction, like a candle snuffed out in an instant.

I played golf on my doorstep or a few miles away at Margherita, where the undulating course wound through the sprawling tea plantations. I swam in a private pool. Once I went off into the jungle on the back of a gently swaying elephant to watch a family of rare white rhinos, which are not really white at all but merely a lighter shade of grey, wallowing in a shallow muddy pool, their own backs the feeding ground for numerous elegant, brilliantly white egrets. The royal Bengal tiger roams this territory but failed to put in an appearance on this occasion, for which I was not sure whether to be disappointed or thankful. An engineer from the refinery kindly took me fishing. We drove into the hills to a spot on a tumbling, crystal clear stream where he taught me, with great patience, how to affix the bait and cast a line. It is tempting to think there is nothing to it, but this is a skill which looks a great deal simpler than it really is. The proof is in the numbers. It was not long before the pupil seemed almost to equal the master in the accuracy, if not the elegance, of his cast, which made it all the more baffling that the fish, dumb creatures, invariably preferred his bait to mine. Why should they be interested in rewarding elegance? Ordinarily I would have dismissed this as pure luck, but surely the luck should have been on my side. After all, I was the beginner. But the evidence in favour of skill was mounting, literally piling up, and the final, unarguable tally stood at: master, plenty; pupil, zero.

In retrospect, given all these outings and extracurricular activities, it is difficult to see quite how or when I managed to fit in the work I had come to do, but it did happen. Somehow I succeeded in dodging the trickiest issues, keeping the inquisitive accountants at bay with the deft use of pseudo-techno-speak, an unforgivable sin, and contriving always to stay a page ahead of the field, to mix my metaphors. I wrote my report, probably in terms designed as much to obscure as to clarify, and they bought it hook, line and sinker, along with a computer to implement it, but of course by then I was several thousand miles away and beyond retribution.

The return journey was not unlike the outward one in reverse. The Fokker Friendship this time bore me downstream above the Brahmaputra without too many alarms, or too many goats, to Calcutta. There, in spite of the minimal effect of my previous encounters, I was prevailed upon once again to engage with my colleagues' tormentors and, so far as I can recall, with similar impact. At least I was able to enjoy another couple of nights, with curry buffet, at the Grand Hotel and a last stroll on the maidan. The story was much the same in Delhi, except that I escaped for a bit of pure tourism to Agra and the Taj Mahal, which is stunning but would be even more so if they exchanged the murky waters of the ornamental lakes for the sparkling blue stuff in the postcards and publicity photographs. There was no cricket to detain me in Bombay so I stayed only long enough to be dined and thanked for my efforts by the Sales Director before I left the subcontinent for good, as it turns out to have been, for I have flown over it but never again landed there in the forty four years since. Pity. I would like to have seen the south of the country, Bangalore and Madras, and perhaps Ceylon before it became Sri Lanka and tore itself apart in civil war. But it was not to be.

Instead of flying direct to London I broke my journey at Rome. There I was very fortunate to be the guest of Flora Mastroianni, the former, or estranged (I'm not sure which she was at that stage), wife of Marcello, who made his name as the hot property of Italian films with his role as the high-living hero of Fellini's *La Dolce Vita*, after which he was off like a shot. I suspect Flora was much too nice and homely, perhaps not glamorous enough, for the new Lothario of the silver screen. She was nonetheless far more sophisticated than I would ever be and in a different social and financial league. (If my reader is silently mouthing accusations of name-dropping here, I can only say that it's about the only name worth dropping in this book, so I shall not apologise.)

Anyway, I had met her a year or two earlier at the bull-running festival of San Fermin in Pamplona and for some reason we had kept in touch. Out of sheer kindness she put me up and entertained me with her friends at smart restaurants and bars in Rome and probably indulged me a little by listening to some of my tales of the Orient.

Then I flew home to London in time for Christmas and a well earned rest from my... well, my holiday in India.

A Rock In The South China Sea

My first taste of living abroad was when I was in the Army in Sierra Leone, about which I have written extensively elsewhere (*Not Half a Life*). Another nine years passed before I left England again for any length of time more than a few months. On this occasion I went entirely voluntarily, to live and work in the crown colony of Hong Kong, as it then was and continued to be until nearly thirty years later when it was handed, with a wish and a prayer that not too much would change, into the tender hands of the People's Republic of China.

Taking advantage of some holiday due to me and the fact that the company was paying my fare, I travelled out in easy stages, spending time first in Greece and then in Thailand. Landing in Athens I made pre-arranged contact with the sister of a friend of mine in London. She had recently married a US Air Force officer stationed in Athens, so I was immediately welcomed into a group of Americans roughly my own age and hell bent on making the most of their good fortune in having such a great posting. I was given a room in someone's flat, thus enabling me to explore Athens during the day while my hosts were working and to join them in the evening for drinks, dinner, a party or whatever was happening. On the Friday of my stay there was a spontaneous decision to fly off to Rhodes for the weekend. It was September, the weather was wonderfully fine and warm and I felt as free as air, with no thought to the new job I was about to start.

After a week or so in Greece I flew on to Bangkok, arriving there at the tail end of a monsoon downpour which caused such flooding that the airport bus drove all the way into town up to the axles in muddy water. By the following morning the flood waters had receded, draining away into the many streams and canals that cut through the city. The company had no business in Thailand but maintained a small office with a watching brief, to keep an eye open for opportunities arising in the market of sufficient potential to tempt us to bid. The office proved to be within walking distance of my hotel so I decided to pay it a surprise visit.

A less determined person, or one with less time on his hands, would have abandoned the search long before I succeeded in locating a door marked faintly with the company name, on the fourth floor of a dingy building doing its best to remain anonymous. I pushed open the door and startled a young girl sitting behind a typewriter painting her nails. At least she was awake. She treated my arrival with the utmost suspicion, even when I explained who I was and why I was there, that is, to pay a social call on a colleague. Still not entirely convinced that I was harmless, she nonetheless got up and opened the door to an inner room, through which I caught a glimpse of a man in a tilting chair with his legs resting on an empty desktop. A whispered conversation ensued, the secretary clearly not wanting to disturb her boss's slumber too abruptly, before she emerged to invite me in. Our man in Bangkok was now fully alert and, sizing up the situation instantly, he greeted me:

'Good morning Peter, nice to see you. Welcome to Bangkok. Please excuse our modest accommodation. We don't have the pleasure of many visitors here. Would you think it's not too early for a little pre-lunch drink?'

'Not at all' I replied.

'Fine. Shall we go then?'

My presence in town was a good excuse for him to get out and about and he evidently enjoyed taking me to some of his favourite little places, as he called them. Since I am such a reluctant tourist I was glad of his company and happy to discover corners of Bangkok not normally frequented by coach parties of foreign visitors.

There must have been someone somewhere in the company's management who was aware of our Bangkok operation, if that is not too positive a word for it, but I suspect that nothing much was expected of it and nothing much was undoubtedly what it achieved. It was hardly typical of our activities in the Far East, which were concentrated on Hong Kong and Singapore, but it was my introduction and an experience I would not easily forget. From Bangkok it was a relatively short hop to Hong Kong, where I arrived in September 1968. I stayed there for two interesting, mostly enjoyable, but sometimes frustrating years.

In so many respects the situation was unreal. There we were, stuck on a rocky little island, a fraction of the size of the Isle of Wight, with access to an area of the mainland far smaller than Hampshire, hemmed in by a fortified frontier patrolled on the Chinese side by heavily armed guards whose duty it was to keep us out and, more importantly, the citizens of the People's Republic of China in. It was a trip of about forty miles by boat west to the tiny Portuguese territory of Macau, notable only for its casinos, which were not permitted in Hong Kong and where poor Chinese, inveterate gamblers that they were, could be seen getting poorer by the minute. Apart from this there was nowhere the Hong Kong resident could go without taking an aeroplane.

The population of five million or so was overwhelmingly (more than ninety-nine percent) Chinese, mostly Cantonese, and permanent. Apart from a few thousand Indians, Japanese and Americans, the rest, perhaps less than thirty thousand, were European, mostly British, and impermanent. The Chinese, being better off than their country cousins across the border and, unlike them, free to use their considerable initiative to improve their lot, lived largely uncomplaining lives, though the year before I arrived there had been communist-inspired strikes, riots and street violence leading to a number of deaths, including several policemen. There was a great variety of cottage industry, much frenetic activity carried out in noisy and sweaty workshops. Some Hong Kong Chinese acquired an education, succeeded in business or a profession and prospered. A few made huge fortunes in, for example, textiles and shipping. The vast majority, however, were poor by European standards, living in grim conditions in enormous, teeming blocks of flats like anthills, each housing numbers equivalent to a medium-sized English town. In fact the entire European expatriate population of Hong Kong could probably have been accommodated in just one such estate, providing of course that they were subject to the same overcrowded, cramped and insanitary conditions as the actual occupants.

By contrast, the Europeans lived in spacious, air-conditioned apartments at various levels on the hill, known as The Peak, that rose steeply behind Central district (in rough terms the higher your status, the higher the level), or in even more luxurious houses on the south side of the island, by the sea. There, for the most part, the housework and usually the cooking were done by a female servant (*amah*), who frequently lived in and was paid a pittance. This allowed European wives to pursue their various social activities unfettered, while their husbands went off to their air-conditioned offices to make large amounts of money which was taxed at a maximum rate of fifteen percent by a paternalistic, unelected and unrepresentative government, comprised almost entirely of British officials pursuing careers in the colonial service.

However much the indigenous Chinese may have benefited from the opportunities provided by the laissez-faire environment, at least by comparison with their compatriots across the border in the republic, it was the colonials who really profited. The long-established businesses which dominated commercial life may locally have been household names (Jardine, Swire and Hutchinson were examples), but they were privately owned companies run by dynastic families in a prevailing culture of secrecy. As private companies they were not obliged to, nor did they, publish detailed accounts and the enormous range of their activities was effectively disguised by the unrevealing names of the diverse organisations they owned. Their tentacles reached into every area of business in the colony and increasingly in the wider markets of the far east, from banking through luxury hotels and insurance to manufacturing, shipping and air travel. If these businesses had been built largely on the backs of cheap, and sometimes sweated, Chinese labour, they were managed, certainly at the senior and middle management levels, almost exclusively by expatriate staff. These men, as they invariably were, might be seen as fairly big fish in a very small pond, many of whom would have struggled to achieve anything like the same status and rewards in the much more competitive market at home. Which I suppose was, in part, why they were there in the first place.

I have always taken it as axiomatic that money-making, as opposed to wealth creation with its implied beneficial social effects, is the supreme raison d'être of Hong Kong. Business is everything. When I returned to Hong Kong for a short visit (yes, on business) in the late eighties, nearly twenty years after I had left in 1970, I made some comment to a government minister about the never-ending process of construction, demolition and reconstruction on the island, with office blocks thrusting ever higher and sweeping over every spare square foot of land. He replied that the day Hong Kong ceased to be a building site would signal the imminent death of the place. Out of a misplaced sense of politeness I didn't ask whether that justified pulling down the Hong Kong Club, the Repulse Bay Hotel and other buildings of either architectural distinction or historical interest. I couldn't avoid the feeling that there was always a whiff of philistinism about Hong Kong.

One thing that I found slightly irritating was the sneering attitude of so many expatriates to Britain, which seemed to me both unreasonable and disloyal. There was a widespread scorn for the United Kingdom, which was the object of constant criticism for its welfare state mentality, its pathetic economic performance and its allegedly socialistic tendencies, no matter which stripe of government happened to be in power. This was a gross exaggeration, even under a Labour government in the late sixties, but some aspects are truer now and I would certainly argue that the UK benefits system has grown to the point of tolerating, if not actually encouraging, an unhealthy state of welfare dependency. In fact the British in Hong Kong struck me as in general profoundly uninterested in politics, which is perhaps all of a piece with the motivations sketched above. They approved of the undemocratic form of rule under which they lived and if the system had permitted them a vote they would have returned by an overwhelming majority any right wing government promising low taxes and minimal interference with their business. Of course I am generalising here, since not all Hong Kong expatriates could be tarred with the same brush and I am sure there were plenty of exceptions, particularly in academia and the media. But I knew quite a few people, born, bred and educated in England, who nevertheless professed a thorough dislike of their home country and who said they would never return to live there. This proved to be no idle threat: on leaving Hong Kong many settled elsewhere, Australia being perhaps the favourite destination.

On my arrival in the colony I was surprised at the almost complete lack of social integration between the British and the Chinese, which I immediately assumed to be the choice, or the fault, of the Brits. This turned out to be far from the case: if anything it was the other way round. Certainly the middle class, educated Chinese appeared to have no wish to mix socially with the 'gwei-loh', the term, meaning barbarian, commonly applied to all westerners. Nor did they, except at the level of the business function, which was probably an obligation tolerated rather than welcomed. As for the rest, the masses, the question did not of course arise. Most

Chinese spoke no English and had little or no contact with foreigners; conversely, I should think the number of Chinese-speaking Europeans could be counted on the fingers of one hand. A number of young expatriates had Chinese girlfriends, and some went as far as to marry them, but for the most part these tended to be somewhat one-dimensional relationships, if that is not too mealy-mouthed a way of putting it, and the girls were rarely if ever of a comparable background and education.

Not everyone, and particularly not long term residents, would agree with the brief thumbnail sketch I have drawn of Hong Kong, much of which is obviously rather subjective, some might even say unfair or, worse, inaccurate. It is just my personal view of the place and yet I am aware that I have presented only one side of the balance sheet. Naturally there is another side, showing far more positive aspects of life on the rock, as I shall hope to illustrate.

When I arrived it took me a while to come to terms with the limitations of the place, but I soon got the hang of it. Most people on contract with UK-based companies, as I was, or making a career with HK-based organisations, had their accommodation provided as part of their remuneration package, which was invariably better than at home, as if Hong Kong was a hardship posting. The opposite was true: while expatriate salaries were higher, the cost of living was appreciably lower. After a short period sharing a flat in the mid-levels, which was where most Europeans lived, I managed to rent a small house on the south side of the island close to an attractive inlet called Deepwater Bay. It was well furnished and had a fine view across the cultivated fields to the busy fishing port of Aberdeen, where the harbour was packed with junks, sampans and open boats of all sizes, so that you wondered how they ever managed to manoeuvre their way back and forth. I acquired a part-time amah who was extremely pleasant and took every opportunity to talk to me about her life, being keen to practise the English she was learning at evening classes. There was a room available for her but she didn't live in as there was no necessity and she was shortly to be married. Anyway, she kept me in good order and occasionally did the cooking, so I felt very fortunate.

Living on the south side of the island, some miles from my office in Central district, would have been impractical without transport of my own. With so many people coming and going, there was an active market in second-hand cars, so before moving in I was able to buy myself a racy sports car, a Triumph TR2, the like of which I could never have afforded in England. On six mornings a week (we worked half day on Saturday) I would drive over the hill and down into town, where I parked on the rough land recently reclaimed from the harbour but not due for development until the settlement was complete, a process requiring several years. For next to nothing a chap would look after the security of the car, a sort of minor protection racket since there was little danger of damage except from him if I failed to pay up. If I gave him a bit extra he would keep the car clean and polished, so I did. It was a good deal.

Our offices were on the fifteenth floor about half way up a mainly glass building on the sea side of the nearest street to the harbour's edge, so that the only thing intervening was the stretch of newly reclaimed land on which I was parked. I didn't like looking out because I suffer from vertigo, but for those who did there was a terrific view north across the water to urban Kowloon, beyond which lay the more rural New Territories and the border separating us all from the Chinese republic. Less than twenty years later the street on which the office was situated had become the third street back from the harbour front and there was no longer a view of any sort from the fifteenth floor, nor even the thirtieth. By chance I happened to stay on the thirtieth floor of a hotel on one of these streets between our old office and the harbour and there were quite a few floors above mine. Yet more land had already been reclaimed for future development, with the effect that Victoria Harbour was steadily narrowing as Hong Kong Island edged ever closer to the mainland. Presumably this land reclamation must have affected the flows and currents in the harbour, which is in fact the busy strait separating island and mainland. I trust the Star Ferry Company, whose boats looped continuously between Central district and Kowloon, were able to hold down their fares in line with the reduction in the crossing. From memory, the fare during my time was 20 cents, though I don't recall whether that was for a single or a return. At roughly 14.5 HK dollars to the pound sterling, it hardly mattered.

Talking of heights, I have suffered from vertigo – a fear of them – all my life. There have been occasions when I tried to conquer this fear by, for example, following a narrow path across a steep mountainside or by daring to look down from one of the lower stages of the Eiffel Tower or by leaning casually on the rail of a Channel ferry's deck. Nothing worked. I was either petrified, unable to move, or I had to fight the urge to fly, the inevitability of the fall. Just picturing such situations causes me to screw up my eyes against the thought. By way of illustration, I remember once lying on a beach somewhere reading a book. Towards the end of

Norman Mailer's novel *An American Dream* our hero, whose wife has just died in a fall from their tenth floor apartment and who is himself suspected of having been responsible for her death, is in his father-in-law's library. He is seized by the impulse to go out onto the terrace, this time thirty floors up, and to walk round the parapet, a foot wide and forty inches above the terrace floor, eighty paces with two right-angle turns to negotiate and a sheer drop of hundreds of feet to the glistening, beckoning wet street below. The agony of this scene stretches out over several pages, culminating in near-catastrophe when the older man pokes an umbrella at his son-in-law, who is saved by grabbing the umbrella and hauling himself back to the sanctuary of the terrace. It was too much for me. I put the book down, my stomach in my mouth. It made no difference that I was at sea-level at the time.

They say that work is the curse of the drinking classes. There was more than a grain of truth in that with regard to my two years in Hong Kong, though I would broaden it to suggest that work tended to get in the way of pleasure, whether or not alcohol was involved. Most of the time I simply didn't enjoy my work. Not for the first time I found success in major sales campaigns to be very elusive, but so did our competitors. A company that seemed like a good prospect would demand detailed technical proposals, take an age to study them and then sit on them, doing little except to pinch any ideas that cost them nothing to implement. Business managers who constantly boasted of their innovation and dynamism in the market were incredibly cautious when it came to investment in new technology and were guilty of seeing the computer as no more than a sophisticated accounting machine and as such an unnecessary expenditure. I found top management to be utterly uninterested. There were always cheaper ways of doing things, usually entailing taking on a few more staff and paying them peanuts. In those relatively early days of commercial computing, trailblazers were very thin on the ground in Hong Kong.

Paradoxically, Government itself was the most extensive and innovative user of computers in the colony. Whereas I was responsible for sales to the private sector, my good friend and fellow Bristolian Roger Ellis dealt exclusively with the public sector. At one point a fiercely competitive battle was raging between IBM and ourselves for the replacement and major upgrading of the principal Government computing facility. One day, not long before the crucial decision was due to be made, Roger picked up the phone to ring one of his Government contacts. He found himself on a crossed line, but instead of cutting the call and redialling, something he would normally have done automatically, some instinct made him cover the mouthpiece and start to eavesdrop on the conversation he had stumbled upon. It turned out to be between two of the key people in the upcoming decision on the Government contract. Roger then listened to a rehearsal of all the arguments for and against the two major bids. By the time he put the phone down he knew exactly what now needed to be done in the final stages of negotiation to sink the competition and clinch the deal for the company. Was there ever a better example of serendipity at play, or rather at work?

For a period of time there were better and potentially more profitable things to do in the office than work. My elder brother Jeffrey, then engaged in climbing the greasy pole at the Stock Exchange in London, sent me a card postmarked Sydney. 'You probably aren't aware' he wrote, or words to that effect, 'that there is mayhem on the Australian markets. Dealing is frenetic following rumours of the discovery of massive new mineral resources. I am out here to assess the position and try to calm things down a bit.' Well, yes. In Hong Kong we were all so unaware that normal business had virtually come to a standstill. Everybody was speculating (betting) on two-cent stocks, on companies that no-one had ever heard of, in the hope that they, the punters, would strike it rich when one of their holdings struck gold, or more likely nickel. We were all spending more time studying the stock lists, with a pin handy, or on the phone to brokers, than we were getting on with our work. A sales commission or a company bonus would pale into insignificance compared to a big win on the market. The first to hit the jackpot were those who picked Poseidon and bought shares at a few cents apiece. They shot up to about two hundred dollars almost overnight. I knew a couple of chaps who became instant dollar millionaires on Poseidon. News of their coup whistled round the colony and for every person disappointed at missing out there were dozens of optimists diving for their brokers' sheets, frantically searching for signs of the next winner. I had a call from a friend who said he was in a syndicate, a member of which had received a hot tip. They had to act quickly. Did I want to join? I would kick myself if I missed the chance: he reckoned it was an absolutely sure bet. The company's name was North Flinders. It was the next share to go ballistic, though in the wave of selling we couldn't get out at the top. Never mind, we made a huge relative profit and took our gains without shelling out a single cent. In the post I received a buying note, a selling note and a cheque for the difference, minus a modest broker's fee. Even so, I was left pondering what might have been. My natural caution had trumped the certain conviction of the friend who had urged me to buy, and instead of going for broke I had wagered a sum well within my means. If I had put my shirt on North Flinders, as several others did, I would not have made a million but I would have been able to afford a few thousand new ones.

A similar thing had happened not long before I went to live in Hong Kong. I was in Dublin with some friends, in theory arranging a rugby tour while actually on a four day pub crawl. We were drinking at McDaid's Bar one day when an Irishman of our acquaintance gave us a tip for a horse running that afternoon. 'A racing certainty' he announced and proceeded, along with my friends, to put all his available cash on the nose. I timidly chipped in a rather trivial sum. The nag romped home out of sight of the field. I won, but couldn't rid myself of the feeling that in reality, and for reasons of cowardice, I had lost. I was clearly never destined to make a fortune, at least not by gambling (and, as it happens, not by any other means either).

One of the best things about working in Hong Kong was lunch. But I must immediately qualify that statement. I am not talking here about long, expensive, alcoholic lunches of the sort where personal relations with customers are developed and consolidated (a reward for services rendered) or which provide the opportunity to cosy up to potential customers (a down payment for future favours). No, I refer to something much more mundane – just the everyday mid-day meal. Except that it didn't happen every day. Sometimes, for whatever reason, I ate a sandwich at my desk. Occasionally I would stroll along to the Cricket Club or the Mandarin

Hotel to meet a friend for a snack or an English-style lunch. Then, maybe two or three times a week, I would go with a colleague to one of the many Chinese restaurants within easy walking distance of the office. There was a huge choice. Cantonese cooking was naturally the most widely available and very good it was too, but my favourite local place was a Shanghai restaurant that operated on four floors, all of which, if you mistimed your arrival by a few minutes, could already be full. It filled from the ground floor up and however early you arrived, it seemed there was never a free table to be had below the third floor. The atmosphere was terrific: bustling, excited, with everyone talking at once, waiters shouting orders to unseen staff, pretty waitresses gliding between the tables laden with exotic dishes which made the mouth water in anticipation. I don't remember whether there was a single kitchen or one on each floor, but the service was prompt and efficient and the food invariably delicious, all the better accompanied by the traditional tea rather than beer or wine.

There were other options. Dim sum restaurants were very popular and unlike anything I have found elsewhere on my travels. I'm not sure how the term dim sum might be translated, but I would describe it as a sort of ambulatory buffet. Waitresses carrying large trays held in place by a harness over the shoulders, a bit like the cinema salesgirls who used to cruise the aisles when the interval lights came up, or pushing multi-decked trolleys, would wend their way between the tables offering a vast array of small dishes, each not much more than a taster. You could try calling them to your table, which would set you in competition with a hundred other diners, or grab them as they passed, which meant that you might end up eating things in an unconventional order – meat, dessert, fish as an extreme example – if you were not prepared to wait for the next logical course to come within hailing distance. This risk of jumbling up different and possibly incompatible tastes was all the greater since often you had only the vaguest idea, or none at all, of what it was you were ordering, even when you could see it in front of you. An enquiry in English would be answered with a completely uncomprehending look and some gabbled Cantonese. The average dim sum restaurant as I remember it covered roughly the area of half a football pitch, with several hundred customers creating a permanent cacophony by simultaneously conversing with their friends at the tops of their voices across large round tables while shouting their requirements at the dozens of perambulating servers. It must have been very tempting for the latter, pulled this way and that by competing demands for their attention, to cultivate a selectively deaf ear. That is certainly how it seemed.

The discovery of real Chinese food, in all its infinite variety, was for me one of the great benefits of living in Hong Kong. Yet, strangely, I have never since enjoyed it. This paradox is easily explained by the fact that Chinese cooking, in the thousands of oriental restaurants to be found in England and indeed elsewhere in Europe, has over the years been modified to suit English and European tastes, so that it no longer bears much resemblance to the original. It may also be that the authentic ingredients are not readily available in the west. In any event the risk has been removed, leaving a uniform blandness. Perhaps this has something to do with the overuse of monosodium glutamate, but I had better not pursue that line as I know no more of chemistry than I do of commercial catering. My suspicions, however, tend to find confirmation in the fact that so many oriental establishments offer a whole range of dishes from Canton, Shanghai, Szechwan, Thailand and Vietnam as if these cuisines were homogeneous. It must be possible to find authentic cooking today in, say, London's Chinatown, but you'd have to know where to go and you had better be dining with a Chinese friend.

On leaving the office in the evening it was easy, and agreeable, to slip into the habit of stopping off for a drink on my way home. I might meet a friend in one of the smart bars at the Mandarin or the Hilton, which was a very pleasant way to pass an hour or two, but it was unlikely to end there. From either hotel it was a short step to the Hong Kong Cricket Club (HKCC), where I could guarantee to run across any number of kindred spirits in the shape of fellow members. San Miguel, the local brew, flowed freely (anyway, cheaply) at the bar of the club pavilion, though gin and tonic was dispensed in almost equal quantities as most people, including me, have a limited capacity for ice-cold fizzy beer. From HKCC I sometimes went to finish the evening at the Foreign Correspondents' Club (FCC) where the conversation, however drunken, was always lively. I was obviously not qualified for membership of the FCC and I've no idea why I should have been admitted in the first place. After a couple of visits I suppose they know your face and nobody thinks of questioning your right to be there. Very occasionally I might drop off at a bar in Wanchai, which was on my way home, but only if my judgement was seriously impaired. The raucous atmosphere, naggingly persistent bar-girls and loud American GIs on R and R (rest and recuperation) from Vietnam were anything but my cup of tea. It must have been at about this time that I adopted the aphorism I have ever since used jokingly as my family motto: *Never eat on an empty stomach*. Unfortunately, more often than not it falls on uncomprehending ears and is met with a blank look. The person who sees the joke is invariably the kindred spirit.

My TR2 was good fun to drive, giving the impression of greater speed than was actually the case, partly because it was open to the rushing wind with the soft top down and partly because the noise of the engine was more roar than purr. Its pre-eminent quality, though, was its ability to navigate its way home late at night with minimum conscious intervention by the driver. I touch wood that in those days, albeit before the arrival of the breathalyser, I was never stopped by the police for erratic driving (or anything else) and I managed to avoid hitting anyone or anything by accident or, for that matter, deliberately.

I have mentioned drinking at HKCC but of course this was secondary to playing cricket there. The club consisted of several teams between which there was no crossover of players, so in effect they were separate clubs-within-a-club. HKCC had two sides in the first division of the league, Optimists and Scorpions, who were both strong and unsurprisingly were great rivals. I played for the former and in the two seasons I was there we came second and third in the league. The cricket in the first division was of a high standard. The Optimists included not only some excellent players but also several fellows with notably successful careers or achievements in other fields. Now that I think of it, the same could be said of the Scorpions.

Our two opening batsmen were both legal men: one the most prolific run-scorer in the whole league who, when I returned on a brief visit in 1987, had risen to

Senior Partner in Hong Kong's most prestigious firm of solicitors; the other a Welsh barrister who became the colony's top judge. At number three was another solicitor, less flamboyant but highly dependable. I remember him scoring a dogged hundred against a strong Army attack which included Colonel Peter Mitchell, who opened the bowling for years for the full Army side and who had been a Captain at Eaton Hall Officer Cadet School when I was a cadet there over a decade earlier.

Next in was the Advertising Manager of the *South China Morning Post*, the main English-language daily paper, who was a brilliant all-round sportsman, one of the best tennis players in the Far East and the Hong Kong Open squash champion. He was also a classy wicket-keeper but only second choice behind the stumps because we had another one with years of experience of Minor Counties cricket for Lincolnshire.

The number five bat was an Aussie, as gritty as they come. Not many years earlier he had been playing for his school, next-wicket-down after Ian Chappell, who was to become one of the most highly rated captains of Australia.

In addition to an all-rounder batting at six we had a couple of big, quick opening bowlers and two off-spinners, of whom I was one. We lacked a leg-spinner for variety. The Scorpions had two, not from any policy but by virtue of the vagaries of recruitment.

Our home ground was a perfect gem, an oasis of green right in the heart of Central district and thus one of the most valuable pieces of land not just in Hong Kong but anywhere in the Far East and perhaps beyond. On the south side stood the HK Hilton, to the north a set of equally tall modern office buildings, while the west side was bordered by the older, lower and more handsome law courts, traditionally colonial in style. There was terraced seating part way round the ground, though it was rarely occupied by more than a thin scattering of spectators, a few drifting over from the hotel, no doubt with time to kill rather than any particular eagerness to watch the Optimists do battle with the Army, say, or the Indian Recreation Club. Sometimes, when ships of the Royal Navy or the US Navy were in port, the stands would be fuller than usual. It would have been quite interesting to know what the Americans made of this strange game which they were almost certainly seeing for the first, and probably the only, time. Sadly, this was all too good to last and soon after I left the colony HKCC was packed off to a new purpose-built ground in the hills, not far from where I used to live, so that more productive use could be made of the Central site. I am not sure whether the pavilion was spared the bulldozer, but it deserved to be, as a haven of calm in the maelstrom of the city centre and as a relic of the charming colonial architecture of the gentler past. The HK powers-that-be, however, not being known for their sentimental turn of mind, are unlikely to have been swayed by such unbusinesslike considerations.

My experience of cricket in the Far East was not limited to Hong Kong. Each year a party from HKCC went on tour to Manila, capital of the Philippines, where a full programme of entertainment was organised, including two or three matches. These were only nominally the main events of the tour, since both sides routinely included at least one or two people who had rarely if ever played the game (Americans and Germans, for example) and, frankly, the result was of no consequence to anybody. The games invariably started late to allow time for the hair of the dog, which may have mitigated the worst of the inevitable hangover but which also started the process leading to the next. Whatever the state of the match, lunch was more important than cricket and usually lasted considerably longer. The menu was simple and unchanging – beer and curry, as much as you liked of each. Matches had to be all-day affairs because if they had been due to start after lunch they would never have started at all. During the afternoon session they normally degenerated into near-farce, with eventually either both sides claiming victory or an honourable draw being declared. It was, after all, only a way of passing the daylight hours relatively harmlessly. Then on with the motley!

At the end of the 1960s the Hong Kong cultural scene was not exactly vibrant, at least not for the European resident. City Hall had been built on the harbour front in 1962 to accommodate libraries, art galleries, a theatre, a concert hall seating fifteen hundred people and exhibition space for trade shows and other promotional events. This sounds impressive but in the context of a city with several million inhabitants it is fairly modest and in reality most of the events it hosted were local and amateur. Official Government literature at the time praised it, and by implication the worthy people of Hong Kong, for its great success as demonstrated by attendance statistics. Mind you, HK Government publications could never be accused of understating its own achievements. I sometimes thought this was the one thing that Hong Kong had in common with the People's Republic.

Chinese opera commanded a large following but I found it excruciating and so, I suspect, did most of the non-Chinese population. The HK Philharmonic Orchestra gave fairly regular performances of the standard repertoire and for an amateur group of musicians it was not too bad, but nothing like a professional outfit. During my two years I can remember no more than a couple of visits by known professional orchestras. I think there were some amateur dramatics and there was certainly an active Gilbert and Sullivan Society. I don't need to rely on my memory to be sure of that, since my wife Helen reminds me that she was an enthusiastic member of the chorus, though I neither knew her at the time nor, to the best of my knowledge, saw her perform on stage. I'm sure there were numerous art exhibitions at City Hall, but I don't recall attending one.

Nobody of my acquaintance owned a television and I doubt if they would have been much tempted to watch it in any case. From what I could gather there was a channel that broadcast pretty well non-stop Chinese opera and if there was a European channel then I have no recollection of it. I definitely remember listening to the radio. Every morning as I prepared to go to work I was tuned in to Radio Hong Kong for a programme of news, current affairs and stories of local interest, a bit like a scaled-down version of the BBC Radio Four *Today* programme which has been running continuously for several decades. The programme had the appealing title of *A Pearl in your Hand* and was very well presented by a young journalist by the name of Cristina Stuart.

One evening in 1969 I went to a party at which I met Cristina, who had tragically been widowed at the age of twenty-five and who came to play a large part in my life over the next ten years or so. She remains to this day a very close friend and her son Freddy, born just after his father's death in 1966 and now an actor living with his American wife and son in Los Angeles, is like a son to me.

As on other occasions when I have worked abroad I took the opportunity to see a bit more of the world on my way home. On my departure from Hong Kong I went first to Taiwan, on the grounds that, since mainland China was a closed shop, this was the only place I could experience a fully Chinese society, that is to say one which was neither subject to colonial rule nor which formed a minority of the population. I did one or two tourist things such as visiting museums and galleries but I wearied rather quickly of endless cabinets of Ming vases and the like. The most memorable aspect of my brief stay was the food. A friend in Hong Kong had given me an introduction to someone with whom he had a strong business relationship and when I made contact I was immediately invited for dinner. This turned out to be a family affair with six or eight of us at table and the conversation at times a little strained as most of them had minimal English and I neither spoke nor understood whatever language they were using between themselves. But the food was sensational and though I can't recall precisely what we ate I can still picture the scene of the meal which consisted of many courses, all cooked and delivered to the table by the businessman's wife who was thus unable to play any social role in proceedings. She produced savouries, shellfish, soup, fresh fish, vegetable dishes, meat courses, pastries and a variety of sweets, which were not necessarily served or eaten in that order, or in any particular order at all. Dishes covered the table and everybody picked at whatever took his or her fancy. It was a veritable feast, the best Chinese meal I have ever had and, no coincidence I'm sure, the only time I was entertained in a Chinese family home.

On another evening I went to a restaurant which

had been recommended to me. It was nearly full but a waiter found me a small table to myself and brought me a menu. This was obviously not an establishment frequented by foreign tourists because no translations were provided, so I was none the wiser.

It was not difficult to indicate my predicament to the owner, who, being a resourceful chap like so many of his compatriots, proved equal to the challenge. Summoning a young lad, perhaps his son, he issued brief instructions, sent him off down the stairs towards the exit and smilingly presented me with a bottle of beer which I would have, but had not yet, ordered. I smiled back, my only way of saying thank you, and settled to a study of my fellow diners, who were Chinese to a man and noisily enjoying their meal in each other's company. Perhaps it was just a false impression they gave that everyone knew everyone else.

Except me, of course...

I was on my second beer, again unrequested, before the boy reappeared, puffing. A moment later the owner proudly presented me with a new menu printed in both Chinese and English. He had clearly sent the boy to another restaurant to borrow one of their bilingual menus. It had taken the boy probably fifteen minutes to run there and back, so it wasn't just round the corner.

After allowing me a while to consider the possibilities the owner, who had evidently decided to take personal care of my needs, returned to take my order. I pointed to several dishes, some of which he noted with approval on his pad while signalling by gesticulation that others were available only down the road. In their place he suggested worthy alternatives by vigorous nodding and facial expressions. The food thus negotiated was absolutely excellent and the whole evening an unforgettable episode.

Next stop was Japan. Landing at Osaka, a large industrial city some 275 miles west-south-west of Tokyo, I wandered purposelessly round Expo 70, intrigued mainly by the discipline and obedience of countless identical groups of Japanese visitors who trotted along behind equal numbers of identifying banners held aloft by their leaders to ensure that none of their charges should become separated and lost in Australia or Argentina or some other part of this microcosm of the entire world. They resembled nothing so much as clockwork toys, the image since conjured up every time I see a group of Japanese tourists. I vaguely knew about Expos because a girlfriend in London had forsaken me for Expo 66 in Montreal, whence to the best of my knowledge she never re-emerged, at least not in Hampstead, though I did receive a postcard telling me what a great time she was having over there.

Expos were vast exhibitions consisting of country pavilions displaying the national character, its culture, industry and commerce, the primary objective being to promote exports. Pavilions would range in size and opulence from the United States, whose exhibit would cover roughly the area of a small country to, say, Mozambique with the equivalent of a modest mud hut. They took place in a different country every four years, like the Olympics or various sporting World Cups.

Quickly tiring of Osaka and Expo 70 I embarked on the cultural trail through cities such as Nara and Kyoto, where all the buildings, if not actually Shinto or Buddhist temples, certainly could easily have been mistaken for temples and the ornamental gardens were so peaceful and spiritual that you had to remind yourself that you were not dreaming, that this was all real, except that there were large groups of visitors trotting along behind their banner-carrying leaders to do the job for you. Kyoto had been the ancient imperial capital of Japan from about 800AD until after the middle of the nineteenth century. It occurred to me that when the modern one was created to replace it, the authorities had saved themselves the bother of thinking up a new name by the simple expedient of an anagrammatical reshuffle of the old one.

Having duly taken the obligatory dose of the country's cultural heritage, I boarded the celebrated bullet train for the anagram, Tokyo. Here it became instantly clear that I had abandoned the spiritual for the temporal, Tokyo being a huge, sprawling, essentially commercial city not so unlike many another major city of the developed world. There were of course differences, characteristics unique to the Japanese capital, but I suspect many of them passed me by. What certainly passed me by were several million trotting Tokyo residents who swarmed like ants, orderly and purposeful in pursuit of their work, their shopping or whatever it was they were about. I had been used to the teeming masses of Hong Kong, but mistakenly thought I had left them behind me; here though, they were better dressed, demonstrably more polite and made an effort to take evasive action instead of forcing you into the gutter to pass them.

Downstairs there were no pavements, no gutters and no traffic, but there was what virtually amounted to another sizable town underground, beneath the streets of Tokyo. Although it was entirely pedestrian, this could not be categorised as a mere shopping precinct. I'm not sure whether people lived down there, but it seemed to contain all the normal town amenities of shops, offices, restaurants, bars, cinemas and so on, and it stretched out over an enormous area. The whole place must have been in some way air-conditioned. The only thing lacking was natural sunlight. Putting all this in the past tense is misleading as doubtless this subterranean city still exists and may have been extended in the intervening years.

Thinking back to my experience in Taipei, I remember wondering how on earth I was going to order food in a restaurant in Tokyo, until I discovered that the Japanese had thought of that too. On display in the window were various dishes, or combinations of choices from the menu. The freshness of these items never deteriorated since they were created in plastic – moulded but never mouldy – and painted in a style more naïve than impressionistic, all the colours a bit too bright. Each was allocated a number in Roman numerals, so all that was required was for the diner to point to the selected digit and hope that it tasted better on the table than it looked in art form in the window. In the event I probably concerned myself more with drinking than with eating while I was in Tokyo, having teamed up with a wandering Yugoslav who was staying at the same hotel and who seemed determined to drink the town dry of beer by the end of his few days in residence. When the time came to leave, I was ready.

Hawaii featured on my itinerary, though of my two day stopover I can recall nothing except that the beaches were even longer and yellower than those of Weston super Mare. Apart from that I don't have any mental picture of those exotic islands. Which is not true of my next port of call, San Francisco. The images I retain, however, could as easily be acquired from any old postcard showing the Golden Gate suspension bridge or the tramcars clinging precariously to the near-vertical streets that climb to the heights of the city almost like a flight of steps. Was it in 1970 still, or yet, the flower-power capital of the USA, with free love being loudly proclaimed if not demonstrated at every opportunity by thin 'students' with long hair and streaming moustaches and looking in urgent need of a shower?

The drive down the coast in a hired convertible was fun but I was disinclined to linger in Los Angeles. I had decided instead to head straight for Las Vegas, to confirm that it was indeed worthy of its reputation and thus of my disdain for its shallowness and brash vulgarity. I wanted to see for myself whether anywhere could be quite as bad as its much trumpeted vices, poor taste and lack of civilised values would suggest.

Well, the short answer was that it measured up, or rather down, to any prior expectation. I stayed in a casino. It called itself a hotel but it was really a casino with rooms and as far as I could ascertain was in this respect no different from any other so-called hotel in town. The balance of commercial importance was such that my accommodation, food and drink cost almost nothing, being simply one means of attracting the punters who were collectively guaranteed to lose large sums of money in the gaming rooms. What was given with one hand was taken back tenfold with the other. 'It's so reasonable' they would declare of the price of lunch as another pocketful of dollars disappeared into the maw of a one-armed bandit. But that didn't count: that was having fun. Just to reach the hotel reception you had to run the gauntlet of a regiment of these machines, all presenting arms like a guard of honour to the gullible guest. Only rarely was the sound of money being inserted, handles vainly pulled and fruit spinning trumped by that of a payout, the tumbling coins making a noise sufficient to give the impression of a good return on investment and encouraging all those nearby to continue throwing their money away. The odds of course are pre-programmed into the machine, probably twenty or thirty to one against the oranges lining up in a row. When they do, after say $25 of excitement, you may win $5 or $10 but, as the management well knows, they go straight back in. You have to be wildly optimistic, more likely crazy, knowingly to take these risks, in which there is no element of skill. Again the management knows best: there is never a shortage of nutcases eager to have a shot.

The hotels have other ways of attracting custom. One is boxing. Caesar's Palace, for example, is a name synonymous with world title fights and it's not the only one. The fans turn up in their thousands to cheer on their man, while the hoteliers are safe in the knowledge that, whoever wins, much gold will come their way, either in celebration of victory or in the hope of raising spirits after defeat. All the big hotels have theatres and all the hotels are big so there is lots of entertainment on offer. I went to a show featuring a very well-known American comedian – well-known, that is, to everyone except me. If Winston Churchill said the United Kingdom and America were two countries divided by a common language, or something like that, then the same goes for humour. While everybody around me was collapsing in uncontrollable laughter I was desperately trying, and failing, to see the joke. Not that the subtlety was beyond me, since there was none. To an Englishman used to a play on words, understatement and self-deprecation it was just very unfunny. What's more, without exaggeration this comic was about eighty and looked every day of it, stumbled over his lines and obviously should have been quietly pensioned off years ago. So my previous view of Las Vegas, as somewhere for people of no taste and less common sense, had been vindicated, but I didn't regret making the detour to prove it.

Time away from crowds and the bright lights was now my priority so I hired a car in Denver and drove out of the mile-high city for a meander around Colorado. This was the perfect antidote to Las Vegas and restored my faith in the ordinary American, if not all mankind. Of course the ordinary Americans in question were of the strictly rural type. Some might, with a hint of superiority, call them rustic, while others, more unkindly, would dismiss them as hick. Whatever else, they struck me as open, friendly people, giving the impression that they were more than content with the country life based on the small towns dotted around this part of the mid-west.

I stayed overnight in those towns, ate heartily in their simple restaurants, attended a cattle market without understanding too much of what went on and, best of all, watched a rodeo that was riotously funny, as I think and hope it was meant to be.

Unintentionally I sometimes found myself the centre of attention, not for anything I did but purely on account of my strange accent. When I explained that I was English they wanted to know more, such as the exact location of England and whether it was a part of Europe or the other way round. I had the feeling that they were less interested in what I said than the way I said it, which tickled them pink.

From the rural mid-western state of Colorado to New Orleans is a big step, both geographically and culturally. I wandered the streets of the French quarter in search of the origins of what is now known as traditional jazz, though I imagine it must have been called something else before it became a tradition. Some of the areas that would have been pretty seedy forty or fifty years earlier were now spruced up, their wooden façades and neat balconies freshly painted in bright colours. The sound of jazz could be heard from cafés and bars and once or twice I came upon live bands but more often the music emanated from record players, amplified for the benefit of the whole neighbourhood. Someone recommended a restaurant, *Chez Jacques*, thus named presumably to imply an authentic French cuisine, so off I went to dinner.

It was not an entirely happy experience. The tenderised steak suited my budget but the waiter seemed to think it impertinent of me to enquire exactly what was meant by *tenderised*. My next mistake was to ask for a large glass of Burgundy without specifying more precisely what I had in mind. What he had in mind was a medium sized glassful expanded to fill a large glass by the addition of an ice cube the size of a small brick. When I said I would prefer, if possible, to take my wine without ice he remonstrated with me, pointing out that all six people at the next table were drinking it 'on the rocks' and they weren't complaining. Under protest he stomped off, returned with a glass which he set down in front of me, and waited for my reaction. He didn't like it when it came.

'This is the same wine with the ice removed. May I please have a large glass of Burgundy that is unchilled and has never seen ice?'

This time, purple with fury, the waiter stormed to the kitchen shouting at the top of his voice 'One glass of Burgundy, large, no ice, repeat no ice.'

The eyes of the whole room swivelled to focus on this strange phenomenon, the man who refused the traditional chunk of ice in his red wine.

It was good to have company in Jamaica, where

I stayed with old friends. They showed me quite a bit of the island, which in parts is spectacularly beautiful. We drove up to Newcastle in the Blue Mountains and sat drinking beer in the early evening, with magnificent views over Kingston, better from a distance than in close-up, and out across the Caribbean Sea. We crossed to the north side of the island, to the quaint old town of Port Antonio in the east and the famous waterfall splashing down the hillside at Ocho Rios.

Overlooking the glorious deserted beach at Negril in the far west we ate fresh papaya and mangoes for breakfast on the terrace before sauntering down to cool ourselves lazily in the bluest of blue seas. The busy resort of Montego Bay, full of middle-aged American holiday-makers of the kiss-me-quick variety, was just a few short miles up the coast, but we might have been on another planet. Before long we had to drag ourselves away from this earthly paradise to make the return journey through the centre of the island via Mandeville, the former principal town, and back down to Kingston in time for my flight home to London after an absence of two years.

From The Med To The Cape

The United Nations Educational, Scientific and Cultural Organisation (UNESCO) has its headquarters in Paris. For a while I found myself negotiating with UNESCO for the purchase of a computer to be installed in the University of Rangoon, Burma. Up to a point it was an interesting project, mainly because I was dealing with an international team consisting of a Frenchman, a Brazilian, two Russians and an Englishman and I had to take account of their different approaches to resolving difficulties. Each was concerned with a particular aspect of the contract and I sometimes felt they were in competition to see who could generate the most legal clauses. They were, after all, bureaucrats of a sort so there was no question of leaving anything to chance: all the 'i's had to be dotted and all the 't's crossed. From my point of view, however, the principal benefit was that it involved frequent visits to Paris and thus the opportunity to do some badly needed maintenance work on my spoken French.

After several months of snail-like progress towards a signed agreement, the time came for a review of the position on the ground in Rangoon, to assess the university's preparedness and draw up an implementation plan. I was looking forward to the trip, which might even have given me a chance to drop in on my old sparring partners in Calcutta, but shortly before the details were finalised there was a sudden change of plan as I was handed an urgent assignment elsewhere. A friend and colleague of mine, who was more or less *au fait* with the situation, took over my tail-end UNESCO responsibilities and was despatched to Rangoon in my place.

That same colleague was to become, a quarter of a century or so later, Managing Director of British Gas and then Chairman of the Automobile Association (AA), unless it was the other way round. But for the moment he occupied a much more humble post in the international division of our company and lived in an office just along the corridor from mine. One fine summer morning he stuck his head round my door.

'Are you doing anything particular this afternoon, Peter?' he enquired. I sensed he had something other than work in mind.

'Nothing special,' I replied, 'I've no commitments.'

'In that case d'you fancy a spin in my old crate?'

'Sure. Give me a shout when you're ready for the off.'

In the car on the way to the airfield somewhere near Kingston upon Thames where his little single propeller plane was parked we discussed where we might go.

'How about Brittany?' I suggested, picturing us sitting outside a café with glass in hand before an early dinner.

'No, that's too complicated, with passports and customs and so on.'

'I wouldn't mind a little jaunt to Devon or Cornwall then.' If we had to restrict ourselves to England, that would still be quite a pleasant place to spend the afternoon.

'Mmm...' He was obviously about to reject that idea too. 'I think maybe we'll head for Blackbush. I know the way.'

As I had no clear notion of where that was, I was happy to agree. So with Biggles at the controls, such as they were, and me sitting directly behind him in a combined space about the size of a child's cot, we set off. Although we were flying it could be argued that we were taking advantage of several forms of transport because we started out following a main road, then switched to a railway which tried to give us the slip by entering a tunnel whose exit was not immediately visible, finally picking up another road that would lead us to our destination.

Coming in to land at Blackbush you cross a main road at an acute angle and a very low altitude. I found it a bit alarming to be overtaken by a Morris Minor family saloon probably doing no more than sixty miles per hour, but I suppose that would explain the fact that on touching down we came to a halt in about fifty yards. Since there is nothing at all to do at Blackbush, my pilot checked in as required by the regulations and we left straight away, taking the same roads and railway in reverse back to Kingston. It had been an escape from the office but I really couldn't see the point of it. The round trip, as the crow flies, had probably been less than forty miles. Owning an aeroplane for outings like that seemed to me rather like owning a Steinway grand yet not having the slightest interest in music beyond playing *Tea for Two* with one finger.

The elsewhere to which I was now assigned was the Mediterranean, with responsibility for managing our affairs in Malta, where I would be based, and Libya.

There isn't a great deal of Malta and Libya is ninety-nine percent sand, so it is not immediately obvious why I should have been required to go down there in a hurry. One reason, though not the main one, which we shall come to in due course, was the increasingly strange behaviour of the incumbent manager. Reports had filtered through that he had been acting rather oddly, not least with regard to the grandiose and completely unrealistic plans he was apparently developing for the expansion of the territory. He was thought to have gone native and to have become a bit of a liability. He was therefore told that it was time for a change and that he would shortly be recalled for a spell in London. This, in his eyes, was tantamount to getting the sack, a prospect that seemed to throw him right off keel. His reaction was to try to drum up support from staff and customers for his remaining in his post, a tactic which not only failed but made matters worse and guaranteed his removal at the earliest possible moment. In the event they didn't even wait for my arrival before pulling the poor chap out, so there was no handover.

As soon as I heard that I was going, I mugged up a bit on Malta, about which I knew next to nothing except its location in the Mediterranean somewhere between Sicily and the North African coast. This has always been of great importance because its strategic position has made it the target of armies and navies on every side throughout its history, from the earliest times. Never mind the island's lack of natural resources (there are few trees and no rivers or streams), if you held Malta you dominated the west-east passage through the Mediterranean. As a consequence the island was much fought over, being held in turn by Phoenicians, Greeks, Carthaginians and Arabs. Admittedly this was all rather a long time ago, even before it was conquered at the end of the 11th century by Roger of Normandy, whoever he might have been. Thereafter it was retaken by Muslim forces and then fell to the Spanish. The Knights Hospitallers, who despite their name and origins in the Holy Land seem to have been a pretty bloodthirsty bunch, took over, although in this case it was not by force but by donation, in 1530 and remained in control, repelling various threats including a protracted attempt at invasion by the Turks, until they were expelled by the French under Napoleon 1 who captured, or recaptured, the place in 1798. They didn't last five minutes, the British taking it in 1800. It was then given back to the Knights Hospitallers, but the Maltese people didn't fancy any more of them and demanded British sovereignty.

Subsequent negotiations resulted in Malta being annexed by Britain in 1814 and it stayed that way until independence in 1964. Throughout those 150 years it provided the British with a strong naval base, and latterly a strategic air base, from both of which the Maltese economy benefited enormously until the closure of the UK naval base in 1979. In the second world war Malta was awarded the George Cross for its fortitude and endurance under heavy attack by Germany and Italy between 1940 and 1942. The concept of a whole nation receiving such an honour is a little hard to grasp, but by all accounts the people are, or at least were, proud of their recognition. These days I should guess they're all too busy catering to the hordes of invading holiday-makers to think much of their wartime exploits. Ship repair is still an important contributor to the economy, but tourism is now by far the largest source of the islands' income, applying not just to Malta but to the other inhabited islands in the republic, the tiny Gozo and the miniscule rock called Comino that lies between the other two.

When I arrived in Malta, however, tourism counted for little, save for the occasional cruise ship that dropped in to Valletta for the day, sending its passengers off to buy tacky souvenirs in the narrow lanes and dark alleys of the old town. In fact, apart from the activity around the naval base, the shipbuilding and repair yards, the place seemed to be half asleep. This was not surprising since the population was largely concentrated in the capital, the rest of the island consisting of not much more than flat bare rock and a few villages. Even so I'm not sure it quite deserved the dismissive description of it given to me on my way there, however much it amused me at the time. We were just leaving mainland Europe behind us and looking down on the blue Mediterranean when the chap sitting next to me asked if I had been to Malta before. I told him I hadn't and asked him what he thought of it. 'Well,' he said, 'Let's put it like this. As we approach, you will be able to see it in the distance, like a small cowpat lying on the sea. And as we get closer, it gets bigger.'

He was right up to a point. It did get bigger, but not much. The whole place measures something like seventeen miles by twelve. There's nowhere much to go and even less to see when you get there, so a day out on the island would be over by lunchtime. I did try to find somewhere interesting to visit, but failed hopelessly, despite the brief promise of villages with names like Rabat and Mdina, both of which could be covered in the space of fifteen minutes. Anyway, I was greeted by somebody or other on my arrival at Luqa Airport and immediately introduced to one of my two principal customers. This was the Finance Director or Chief Accountant, I forget which, of the largest British shipbuilder and repairer, with a major dockyard facility at Valletta employing thousands of Maltese. He hadn't come to buttonhole me, to give me an ear-bashing about problems with their computer or the parlous state of relations between our two companies. No, it was quickly apparent that he was there to check me out for my own qualities, primarily as someone he could depend on to join him for a few snifters at the end of a hard day's work. For our first meeting we dispensed with the day's work and proceeded straight to the bar of my hotel, where he tried to convince me that the greatest gift to mankind was bourbon, specifically Jack Daniels, which was his regular tipple. If I had declined his suggestion and opted for a glass of orange juice I think our commercial relationship might have been plunged into crisis before I had unpacked my suitcase. As it was, I explained that I had experienced an irreversible revulsion to whisky, or anything like it, after drinking a great deal of the stuff in Sierra Leone over a decade earlier, but I'd be happy with a gin and tonic. And in the event, several.

My other main customer was one of the big four UK Clearing Banks, which may have been the source of some of the complaints against my predecessor. Whatever else he did wrong it certainly wasn't excessive drinking that offended them, because he was teetotal. Whether or not the managers at the bank indulged I can't specifically recall, but, Malta being the sort of place that could readily drive a man to drink, the odds were against moderation. In fact I remember nothing at all about them as people or as customers, save that there had been some vague dissatisfaction with our conduct of their account which seemed to be resolved at my appearance on the scene, though I think it unlikely that was the result of anything I actually did. Our senior management in London were very keen that the installation in Malta should be seen by the bank as a notable success, which might influence matters in our favour in their larger computing decisions at home. For those of us nearer to the coalface this was a case of optimism bordering on cloud-cuckoo-land. We knew that Malta was a drop in the ocean.

So far so good. All was quiet on the Maltese front: the bank was happy and our man at the shipyard had a dependable drinking partner for the interlude between work and dinner, a variable feast, at home with his wife, who wasn't averse to the odd tot herself. What that left to occupy all the hours of the working day I can't imagine. In any event, with peace reigning on the island it was soon time to make war across the water.

Like Malta, Libya has had a pretty chequered career. It is a vast country, roughly seven and a half times the physical size of the UK, a large part of which is in the Sahara desert, the rest consisting of bare stony plains and scrub-covered hills. There is a narrow strip of land along part of its coastline which has a Mediterranean climate and is therefore cultivable. Libya has a tiny population relative to its size of about 5.5 million, probably no more than about 4 million at the time of which I write, practically all of whom lived on the coastal strip. The economy is dominated by the production and export of crude oil and some of its derivatives. In its history it has been colonised by the Romans, conquered by the Arabs, occupied by the Turks, annexed by the Italians and administered by the French and British. As if that wasn't enough it was heavily fought over in the second world war, then placed under military government by the Allies before becoming an independent monarchy in 1951. That proved to have been a false dawn because King Idris was overthrown by radical Islamic Army officers in 1969. (At the mention of King Idris I can't help thinking of a soft drink of that name, advertised at the time under the slogan 'I drink Idris when I's dri', though it is highly improbable that the one inspired the other.) Thereafter the country emerged as a hard-line socialist state whose primary aim appears to have been the perpetration and active support of Arab and Muslim fundamentalist terrorism. Its leader was Colonel Muammar Qaddafi, considered by some to be charismatic, by others an out-and-out nutcase. He was in charge when I went to the capital, Tripoli, about a year after the uprising and he is still in power as I write, forty years later.

I went there to visit the site of two of our computers, installed on a rental basis in one of the government ministries. What I found was, by any standards, a rum set-up. There was a manager of the department who spoke English (a necessary qualification for someone in his position) and seemed to know his onions. That is to say, he was trained and competent in systems analysis and programming. A good thing too, for he himself did everything that had to be done in the department, save the actual hands-on operation of the machines. For this there was an absurdly large team of operators. There was an even more absurd and larger group of people, all men, who were in theory responsible for systems design and programming. In practice they were all virtual strangers to both disciplines. They turned up to work each day and sat at their desks, perhaps twenty to thirty of them, in a large bare room resembling a basic school classroom. Some just sat, others read comics, while a few flicked through the pages of computer text books as if searching for instant enlightenment. Allegedly they were the cream of the graduate output of the University of Tripoli.

Maybe this situation should not have come as a surprise to me. These men had received their training in England at one or other of the company's education centres. Well, no. It would be truer to say that these men had been sent to England for training, which is not quite the same thing. In London we had a chap, a most genial fellow, whose job it was to look after overseas customer staff, mainly from the Arab countries in which we operated, when they came to the UK for training. He would make sure that the appropriate courses were booked, accommodation arranged and travel organised. In addition he would meet them on their arrival and take them on a little welcoming tour of Head Office. At the end of their tour each student would be given a brown envelope containing an allowance, in cash, to cover any unforeseen incidental expenses that might otherwise have caused them embarrassment, as our man would have put it. But he knew the form.

On completion of their introductory session they would disappear into London's West End and in many cases would not reappear until their scheduled return home, having been nowhere near any company premises in the interim, unless it was to seek additional funds from their fairy godfather at Head Office. These extracurricular costs were of course anticipated and more than adequately covered in the computer rentals charged.

Back in Libya there was business, of a sort, to be done. The only staff we kept in the country were two engineers who were responsible for the maintenance of the computer hardware. We had no sales representation and I was not expected to do anything in that regard during my visit. I was there to solve a problem that was growing with every day that passed. In brief, the Libyans were not paying their bills and it was my job to make sure that changed; in particular, to extract from the government at least a decent proportion of the millions of pounds they owed us in back rentals. I first broached the subject with the computer manager, knowing that he would have no authority in the matter, but wishing to be seen to be observing the niceties. He quickly arranged an interview with the minister and accompanied me the following day to his palatial suite of offices, where I was received like some visiting bigwig.

I had no experience of negotiating with an Arab of any sort, never mind a senior government official close to a military dictator President (neither was there on account of his success at the polls) with a reputation for ruthlessness and no love for westerners. My diplomatic skills had not been honed at the Foreign Office. So, after the preliminary pleasantries, I dived in. I told him that my company was pleased to provide our services to his government but that, unless those services were deficient in some way, he had an obligation to pay the charges agreed in the contract that existed between us. He consulted the computer manager in Arabic, presumably to enquire about his health or perhaps the health of the installation, then turned back to me. In the event of continued non-payment, I said, we would be obliged to take action to restrict their usage of the computer. I indicated a deadline forty-eight hours ahead.

Without giving me a specific commitment, he said something to the effect that I should leave the matter with him and shook my hand with a parting smile. I returned to the department and advised my engineers of what I had done and, more importantly, what I was proposing to do. They were not comforted and far from optimistic as to the outcome. They did not like what I was going to ask them to do.

For the next couple of days I mooched about, with nothing particular to do. I wandered through the main part of Tripoli near my hotel and had a look at the souk. In that post- revolutionary Libya there were no tourists and hardly any foreigners to be seen, so as a European I felt very conspicuous on the street, as if I was constantly under observation. The deadline passed and London confirmed to me that no money had been received. I instructed the engineers to pull the plug, that is, to disable the computers by the removal of a single critical part, and advised the manager, who I had the feeling was broadly sympathetic while obviously unable to say as much.

The result was dramatic. Within twenty four hours London called to tell me that the full amount outstanding had been transferred to our bank account and that I should therefore reinstate the system without further delay. The engineers had the machines operational again in a matter of minutes and no doubt the minister was informed equally quickly. If I had learned little else, I now knew that I had hit them where it hurts, not in the wallet but in the disruption of the flow of information, for it seemed to me obvious that the computers must have been deployed on more important business than mere departmental accounting. But this was not a subject I was interested in exploring. The tensions of the last few days had dissipated. There was relief all round.

My mission accomplished, I was delighted to be on the plane back to Malta the following day. I had been in Libya less than a week, but it felt like a great deal longer. Very soon afterwards a permanent manager for

Malta and Libya, a local man educated at university in England, was appointed and I was able to return to London. Just one aspect of this whole affair struck me as rather odd. Since my primary objective in the Mediterranean had been to resolve the financial problem in Tripoli, why had the company not simply despatched somebody directly from London to do the job, perhaps the Financial Director of our international division? Was this another case, as so often in my career, where I thought I was being asked to do a job for which others were far better qualified? Had I been a bit of a mug to accept an assignment to an unfriendly country in the throes of consolidating a military dictatorship after a *coup d'état*, with all the attendant dangers inherent in such a situation? Not that I was complaining, now that the whole thing was over.

When I was in the Army doing my national service about a dozen years earlier, I had spent the greater part of my two years in Sierra Leone on the west coast of Africa, the white man's grave. (This period is covered in detail in my memoir *Not Half a Life*, published in 2009.) It never occurred to me that I might one day return and it would be misleading to suggest that, in any real sense, I ever did. Like a migrating bird I touched down on my way south.

I had been in Canada for six weeks and was heading for Chile, having broken my journey for a few days in London over Christmas. My recollections of this spell working in Canada are extremely hazy, to the point that I am no longer clear why I was there at all. No doubt it had something to do with the fact that our Canadian company was struggling to achieve any progress in the market, but this was hardly new and in any case what difference could I make in a few short weeks, or even long ones? We were a British company with very limited resources trying to compete against huge American suppliers in their own backyard. To make matters worse, we had recruited a senior IBM executive as Managing Director on a remuneration package which itself consumed a substantial proportion of the overall budget. He ran the show as though he'd never left IBM, spared no expense, especially with regard to his personal comfort and convenience, and seemed not to be familiar with the old adage about cutting your coat according to your cloth. In short, he was quickly running the company into the ground. We fired him soon after my visit, but by then much of the damage had been done and, to rub salt into the wound, the termination of his contract of employment cost us a further small fortune.

Our number two man in Toronto was a nice, laidback Englishman in his mid-fifties. He met me at the airport on a cold Friday afternoon in November and took me to my hotel to check in before putting in a brief appearance in the office. The hotel was on one of those canyon-like streets, ruler-straight between rows of tall buildings broken only by other streets crossing it at right angles. It was like a wind tunnel and a gale seemed to blow continuously down it, directly from the arctic circle. I later decided it was the coldest place in the whole city. In the car my colleague asked if I had anything planned for the weekend. I said it was my first visit to Canada and since I knew nobody here I supposed I would explore the town a little. He then enquired if I liked rugby and when I said I was very keen and had played for a London club until about three years before, he invited me to join him and his wife for lunch next day, followed by a cup final match in which their son was playing. The game took place at a ground on the outskirts of Toronto on which there were probably half a dozen pitches used by a number of clubs who shared a central, timber-built clubhouse. This was a large building on three floors with all the usual facilities, including a spacious bar evocative of many a rugby club at home. Barely had we installed ourselves with our first pints of the evening (our man's wife having agreed to drive back) before someone tapped me on the shoulder.

'Hey, Pete, what the hell are you doing here?'

Within a couple of minutes there were three others, all of whom I had played either with or against in London. Where rugby is concerned, you could say it's a small world. Later my host reminded me that I had said I knew nobody in Canada.

'Well,' I replied, 'I didn't *know* I knew anybody.'

After a while I moved on to Montreal, where we also had a sales office. By now we were into December and it was colder still, with several inches of snow that would almost certainly remain on the ground for the rest of the winter. The locals took this in their stride and normal life, including travel, seemed little affected. I found Montreal a more interesting and attractive city than Toronto and I liked the fact that it was bilingual and showed the influence of both English and French cultures.

In the office the first person I met was an English chap who had been in the same graduate intake as me nearly ten years earlier. We had gone through our initial training together. Now he was married with children and a slight but detectable Canadian accent. Montreal was home. I hit it off well with our manager there and he was excellent company in the hour or two between leaving work and heading off home to his family. We would normally go to one or other of his favourite bars, where the temperature inside would be about thirty degrees higher than outside. He introduced me to the Martini Dry, the genuine article which I firmly believe is only to be found in North America. It had a habit of hitting you between the eyes as you stepped out into temperatures of minus ten or fifteen. I'm not sure what, if anything, I contributed to the business in Toronto and Montreal, but it was fun while it lasted.

There was hardly time to draw breath in London before I was off again, this time to Chile, which is a long way, in every sense, from Canada. I flew British Caledonian to Santiago, via Freetown and Buenos Aires. We stopped for refuelling and a chance to stretch our legs at Lungi, a short trip across the bay from the capital of Sierra Leone, and it was clear to me that not much had changed. The airport buildings were the same ramshackle collection of huts through which I had passed on leaving for Dakar, up the coast in Senegal, over twelve years earlier. The country had by now been independent for almost ten years and the deterioration was evident without going further than the airport. Staff were offhand, uniforms were ragged and dirty and cold beer or Coke was produced for us transit passengers from the same rusty old kerosene-driven fridges. Air conditioning was non-existent, so the contrast between midwinter London, not to mention Quebec, and sweltering Freetown was extreme. I had had a certain affection for Sierra Leone, but now it wasn't nostalgia that I felt, just a slight sadness.

A pattern was becoming evident in my business travels: it was more travel than business. In the southern Mediterranean my work had taken me to a vast country in which we had a single solitary computer installation.

True, in this case it had yielded important financial results. I had nearly gone to Rangoon in Burma, a country in which we had hitherto had no presence and where we were unlikely to build on the UNESCO-sponsored contract, since the place was poverty-stricken and virtually a closed state. Our involvement in the Canadian market was limited, low-key and not notably successful; those adjectives would have been equally applicable after my visit as before it. And now I was heading for South America, a huge geographical region where we didn't operate at all. Where next? Would I be asked to sell igloo-friendly computers to the Eskimos, or punch card systems to a remote tribe of pygmies up the Amazon?

The Chilean episode was from the outset a rather strange affair, with a distinct aura of cloak and dagger. In London we had been approached by a young man claiming to speak for the government of Chile, who wished to discuss the possibility of our supplying them with some very large systems indeed. They knew almost as little about us as we knew of Chile. I was deputed to deal with this chap and we had a number of meetings at which he provided minimal information on the project and I gave him few details of what we might be able to offer, partly because I had been asked to be cautious but not least because I didn't know. If I was cagey, he was even more so, stressing the secret nature of these talks and, to underline this, speaking in a whisper, as if he feared my office was bugged. Maybe I should have done more, or at any rate some, research into the political situation in Chile but, frankly, nobody expected anything to come of this contact, so I suppose I did the minimum necessary.

When, later, an invitation arrived out of the blue for a representative of the company to visit Chile for discussions on the specific terms of a possible contract, nobody quite knew how to react. There was still a considerable scepticism that anything useful would result, but since there was also a counter view that perhaps we were pushing at an open door it was decided that someone should go and furthermore that someone should be me. Once again, it struck me as odd that the company should wish to be represented in these negotiations by a person who had never dealt with governments of any sort, whether local or national, if we exclude the supranational UNESCO, and who was certainly not a technical whiz capable of talking nanoseconds. My main qualification seemed to be that I had been to plenty of distant locations before, had never got lost en route and thus far had not blotted my copybook in my dealings with difficult or dodgy foreigners. Perhaps I was considered, before the expression had actually been coined, a safe pair of hands.

Of course the whole thing was political (another area in which I had no experience). Not that I cared as the plane hung over the Andes, with glorious views of the rugged spine of the mountains to north and south as far as the eye could see, before dropping down to the narrow plain on which Santiago, my destination, lay in bright morning sunshine. In mid-afternoon I set off for an exploratory tour of the town. It was quickly apparent that, despite a lot of once fine public buildings on handsome broad thoroughfares, the city wore a run-down air. There was an urgent need for maintenance and everywhere could have done with a lick of paint. Further evidence of the dire economic situation was clear when I arrived for dinner in the top floor restaurant of my hotel, having ascended in the only functioning lift out of three. I was surprised to find myself the sole diner.

A waiter brought a menu in English which I studied carefully before ordering a beef dish as main course.

'Sorry, sir, no beef,' said the waiter with little hint of anything out of the ordinary.

'Perhaps the lamb?' I ventured, but this time the response was more definitive.

'No meat available today, sir.'

'Right, I'll try the rabbit then.' This must surely be a safe bet, unless the whole population had been wiped out by that dreaded disease that had swept through Europe. But no, I could see the look in his eye. 'Chicken?' My request was declined with a weary shake of the head. 'Maybe you could just tell me what is available please.'

'Fish,' he said, visibly perking up.

'OK, any choice?' I hardly dared put the question.

'Boiled fish, sir.'

'Thank you very much.' At least it came with potatoes, but I hadn't enquired in case I discovered the default option was a chunk of yesterday's dry bread. There was wine, of poorish quality, on tap, so to speak, without the need for lengthy negotiation: a simple question of red or white.

Chile had not always been in such a parlous state.

This extraordinary country stretches nearly 2900 miles from north to south with an average width of just 100 miles from the Pacific Ocean to the high Andes, which straddle the 2500 mile border with Argentina and the shorter one of 400 miles with Bolivia. Its northern neighbour is Peru. Chile was colonised by the Spanish in the middle of the sixteenth century, when Santiago was founded. It gained its independence in the early nineteenth century when the splendidly named Bernardo O'Higgins joined forces with the Argentine liberator José de San Martin to cross the Andes and defeat the Spanish in a series of major battles, none of which is much remembered outside Chile. The colourful Bernardo, by the way, was the illegitimate son of the even more exotically titled Ambrosio O'Higgins, who had earlier been Governor of Chile when it was a Spanish colony. It is difficult, therefore, to imagine that father and son saw eye to eye politically, but at least Bernardo had the decency to wait until O'Higgins senior was dead before launching his bid for independence, which otherwise may well have involved an act of patricide. So O'Higgins junior became the first President of the republic, but his ideas for reform were too radical for local tastes and he was given the order of the boot after five years.

One hundred and fifty years later when taking my first look at Santiago I strolled down Avenida O'Higgins and admired the impressive statue at the bottom, without quite recognising who was being commemorated. I soon rectified that but I still don't know the history of the Dublin connection, or whether his direct descendants eventually abandoned politics for professional snooker.

The considerable wealth of the country had been based on the rich deposits of copper and natural nitrates in the northern Atacama desert, but as the latter started to be replaced by synthetic substitutes between the wars Chile's economy became over-reliant on world copper prices with the result that there was a protracted post-war period of political and social instability. This led to the election as President in 1970 of the democrat Salvador Allende, the first Marxist ever to be elected leader of a state by popular vote. He tried to introduce a radical programme of nationalisation and land reform but was frustrated by a combination of inflation, the flight of capital and a massive balance of payments deficit and was hit hard by the hostility of the USA to his regime.

All this accounted for the crumbling infrastructure, a near-worthless currency, the poverty of choice in my hotel dining room and for my very presence in Santiago. I was there because Allende's administration could not, and in any case as a matter of policy would not, buy computer systems from the hated Americans, as they had always done in the past. Britain and Chile were old friends and allies, so they naturally turned to us for help. Somehow, in spite of our commercial reservations and our close political alignment with the United States, we were prepared to give it a shot.

I had been there for no more than a couple of days when, before I could be brought down by starvation, I succumbed to a particularly nasty bout of fever. This laid me so low that I had to be diplomatically rescued, so to speak, from the hotel and delivered into the arms of the wife of the First Secretary at the British Embassy, who took me home, tucked me up, made me comfortable and ministered to my every need for the next week – well, nearly every need – until I was fit again for active service and could return to the delights of the hotel. This was not as bad as you might think because from now on I was either invited out for dinner or I managed to find some other restaurant where what was actually available bore a passing resemblance to what appeared on the menu.

Restored to health, I embarked on a series of meetings to discuss the technologies we were able to offer, as well as the prices and terms of business on which they could be made available. With regard to the former my strategy, as always, was to be as vague as circumstances would allow while asserting that our computers would satisfy their every requirement short of miracles. As to the commercial aspects of the negotiation I had been fully briefed before leaving London and in general took a hard line, on the assumption that they had nowhere else to go. They say you should never kick a man when he's down, but on the other hand, when better? All this talk led to an agreed provisional equipment specification and an early draft contract document which were sent off by diplomatic bag to minimise delay. Thereafter I was directed to return to London, having achieved, as viewed from the ivory tower, everything that could be done on this first visit. The matter was, at least for the time being, out of my hands.

During my stay I had not managed to see very much of Chile outside Santiago, although I did go to the coast, some sixty miles away, to the port of Valparaiso and the nearby resort town of Viña del Mar. They were not exactly prospering at the time either. I had no stomach for the twenty-two hour flight home, so booked a ticket via Rio de Janeiro, where I stopped off for a few days.

Rio used to be the capital of Brazil until about 1960 when the country's administration was transferred to the new, purpose-built city of Brasilia, which is probably a tourist-free zone. Any amount of tourists can lose themselves in Rio, however, because there is a resident population of over five million, most of whom seemed to me to be either playing football on the beach or celebrating something or other on the streets with great gusto and a lot of noise, although I was a bit early for carnival. Maybe they were rehearsing.

The city is quite spectacular, particularly its backdrop, the skyline with its ring of hills from which the two dominant rocky peaks, Sugar Loaf Mountain and Corcovado, protrude. I went to the top of the Corcovado to see the massive, much photographed statue of Christ, for which Rio is probably best known by those not lucky enough to have been there, and to admire the magnificent views over the bay. The downside of this ascent is that on the way you are brought rudely face to face with some of the most squalid of Rio's numerous slums. I also spent time on the beaches, which run for miles and host endless games of football, some of which I was assured are serious club matches. When I felt I had been adequately rewarded for exertion expended and privation endured in Chile, I caught the plane back to a damp, chilly London.

Unfortunately the Chile affair, so promising at one stage, never got off the ground. In view of the depressed state of their economy, their low credit rating and the continuing political uncertainties, our Ministry of Trade and Industry, or whatever it was called at the time, refused to issue an export credit guarantee, which was an absolute prerequisite of any such overseas contract. In retrospect it seemed remiss of the company not to have checked that out in advance and thereby saved the cost of my trip to South America. So although my missionary work had been effective in the field, it was ultimately to count for nothing in the order book. Perhaps, as it turned out, this was no bad thing. A year or so after my visit the Chilean government was overthrown by the military in a coup led by the notorious General Augusto Pinochet, in the course of which President Allende was killed, along with thousands of others. Ten percent of the population emigrated. For the next decade and a half the dictator Pinochet maintained a repressive regime under which many of its political opponents were permanently 'disappeared'. It was undeniable that I was falling into the habit of involvement in some pretty unsavoury places. Was the company trying to tell me something?

*

Before my adventures in Canada and Chile I had been despatched to West Africa as stop-gap manager, filling in for the regular incumbent, a friend who had been a member of my team when I was an oil specialist responsible for the BP account. Not surprisingly in my view, things had got him down a bit and he was going on extended home leave to rest and regain his sanity. Fortunately I was not there long enough to lose mine.

Nigeria is the most populous country in the whole of Africa, with over one hundred million inhabitants belonging to hundreds of different tribes and ethnic groups. Its history is so chaotic as to be almost incapable of summary, save to say that it encompasses colonialism, slavery, civil and intertribal warfare, wholesale tribal massacre amounting to genocide, military coups, regional secession, brutal dictatorships, religious violence, national wealth from oil, the squandering of oil wealth and the odd small dose of democracy which never seems to last long before the next coup. Others better informed than I am could probably add to that list of atrocities. Corruption at every level of the system is, and I imagine always was, endemic. If I were to list all the countries I have lived in or visited in order of my preference, I would find it easiest to start at the bottom.

Our main office was in Lagos, then the capital city but since replaced as the administrative hub by the newly constructed town of Abuja, which is situated right in the centre of the country, presumably for symbolic as much as practical reasons. In addition to its many other unattractive qualities, Lagos has a horrible climate, very hot and humid, which accentuates the feeling of suffocation induced by the crowded, dirty and smelly conditions typical of downtown areas including the business district in which we had our offices. During my brief sojourn I found no opportunity to visit other parts of the country. This was a pity because there are huge variations in terrain, climate, vegetation and no doubt the character of the people. There is, for example, a central plateau rising to about six thousand feet which I imagine makes it a much healthier place to live, and further north towards the border with Niger the land is a virtual desert supporting little more than thorn scrub. Thus when I have written in derogatory terms about Nigeria, as at the end of the previous paragraph, I really mean Lagos, though reference to the historical shambles applies to the whole country.

It is not difficult to recall a few more pleasant aspects of my time in Lagos, neither will it take long to recount them. I lived in a single storey house in the best suburb. It was suitable for a large family whereas I was alone, so I rattled about a bit. The house was guarded at night and there was a cook and a maid in attendance. A car was at my disposal and, more importantly, a driver, since I would not like to have had an accident or any sort of incident while driving myself. The golf club was not far away. This was essentially somewhere to escape from the hassle of life in Lagos, rather than a great place to play golf. The course had one strange characteristic that remains unique in my experience: instead of greens, it had browns. Where there would normally be close-cropped fine grass there was just soil, rolled out to create a uniformly firm flat surface and then oiled to give it a slickness not entirely unlike the quality of a conventional green. There were no slopes or undulations, however, and the overall effect could hardly be said to be aesthetically pleasing. It was rather odd to hear someone in the locker room despairing at missing a tiddler on the eighth brown. If I ever knew the reason for having browns in place of greens, then I have long ago forgotten it.

Sailing was another activity that had its enthusiasts amongst the expatriate community, sharing with golf the advantage of allowing you to 'get away from it all'. I was taken out in the bay on one occasion by a very attractive girl whose captive proximity and skimpy shorts made it a most enjoyable afternoon, but I am not sure whether, in her eyes, my social skills made up for my complete lack of technical ones. In any event nothing came of it, the sailing or the girl. Although I like the sea, it was nearly forty years before I went sailing again, as a treat just after my seventy-first birthday. This time I suffered the ignominy of being brushed aside by an eighty-one year old when I attempted to make myself useful by assisting with the Genoa in some routine tacking manoeuvre. My humiliation stopped only just short of being sent downstairs to make the tea.

Working in Lagos was not my idea of fun. Being merely the temporary occupant of the manager's seat, I concentrated for the most part on keeping things on an even keel, ready for the return of a refreshed colleague. Far from going for glory, I soon met an inglorious end. Most of the staff were pretty average by the standards I had known elsewhere, but they were relatively well paid and would have been pushed to find comparable positions in the local employment market, so they valued their jobs and showed some interest in promoting the success of the company. I kept a close eye on things such as expense claims, to ensure that nobody thought they could play fast and loose with the system in the regular manager's absence. Minor fiddling almost certainly happened, but I discovered that one member of staff in the accounts department was a serious and serial offender. When it first came to my notice I warned him. The second time I fired him. Oh dear. Nobody had told me this chap was fire-proof. Nobody had told me that his uncle was the Minister of the Interior, to whom he went hot-foot to report that I was working illegally, not being in possession of a valid work permit, which was true though naturally not something I had publicised. Justice, if that is the right word for it, was summary, swift and decisive: I was arrested, given a short time to put some clothes in a bag and bundled onto the first flight out to Accra.

I suppose I should have been thankful to have avoided a worse fate, such as indefinite incarceration in a filthy jail cell with a dozen petty felons, but there's no denying that it was a shock. Once I was safely on the plane and had convinced myself that the situation was recoverable and that I could work from Accra, I started to take a more measured view of the affair. First, I was not personally at fault since it was the company's responsibility to procure me a proper authorisation to work and my director in London had decided to take a calculated risk, given the long delays in processing applications within the Nigerian system. Doubtless I could have declined to go without a permit, on the grounds of both illegality and recklessness, but in truth I didn't really give it much thought. Secondly, I didn't like Lagos and was privately quite relieved to see the back of it.

As soon as I arrived in Ghana I felt better. The first thing I did was to introduce myself at the office and arrange for the senior salesman in Lagos, who would look after things there on a day-to-day basis, to come to Accra with the rest of my personal belongings and to sort out a modus operandi. In fact the distance between the two cities is only about 250 miles, so there was no problem in his coming to see me whenever the need arose, which could be at his instigation or mine. Then I checked in to a hotel and went out for a walk.

Throughout the continent of Africa history is littered with tribal conflicts, wars between neighbours which in general Europeans, or for that matter any outsiders, have difficulty in disentangling. Ghana was no exception, though it does appear to have had a less complicated past than that of Nigeria, perhaps because of the numerical dominance of the Ashanti over much of the territory inland. The Portuguese and the Danish were early traders with the area and from the sixteenth century onwards it was a centre of the slave trade. British influence grew steadily through the eighteenth and nineteenth centuries and after two wars with the Ashanti they occupied their then capital of Kumasi, about a hundred miles inland from Accra, and established the colony of the Gold Coast in the 1870s.

In the first half of the twentieth century economic growth and an education system based on the successful mission schools produced a relatively sophisticated population which started to press for home rule. Following World War II, in which many Ghanaians served with the Royal West African Frontier Force (in which I later served), serious riots in Accra led to constitutional talks and in 1957 the Gold Coast became the independent Republic of Ghana under the leadership of Kwame Nkrumah. It was the first British African colony to achieve independence. In the well established tradition of British colonial history, Nkrumah had been imprisoned for sedition before becoming Prime Minister and then President. He created a one party state and in 1964, again in the manner typical of rulers of newly independent African countries, declared himself President for life. Ousted by a military coup when he was out of the country in 1966, he died in exile in 1972. There were successive coups and counter-coups during the 1970s, so it is hardly surprising that I can't remember exactly who was in power during my sojourn.

Anyway, Accra was a lot more relaxed than Lagos and I literally felt I was breathing fresh air for the first time in months. The city was more open and less oppressively dirty, noisy and crowded than Lagos. I liked the seashore, near which there were a number of once impressive structures built to the greater glory of Kwame Nkrumah and by now either fallen into disuse or never having had any practical purpose in the first place. The difference between monuments, including statues of so-called statesmen, in an African city and a European one is that in Africa they are normally erected by the person being commemorated at the beginning of his rule rather than by a grateful people after its end, in the certain knowledge that by then nobody will want to be reminded of the tyrannical bastard. Fortunately most of the heads of government, or whatever you want to call it, in both Nigeria and Ghana were so quickly overthrown that they had no time to build their own monuments, otherwise there would be no room to move in either Lagos or Accra.

The company's interests in Ghana, if not actually limited to Accra, were certainly centred there and, as in Nigeria, I did not manage to get much beyond the capital. Our man in Accra, nominally a salesman supported by a small team in the office, was a bit of a wide-boy, clever, devious, manipulative, undoubtedly dishonest but energetic and decidedly in the know – altogether a lovable rogue. He had the character and approach of an entrepreneur, a deal-maker rather than a salesman. Here was a man to whom corruption was second nature, who treated the rest of the staff as his personal servants, there only to do his bidding while he was out and about developing profitable relationships: that is, profitable to himself and sometimes, by happy coincidence, to the company as well. I could not swear that the company's business was his main occupation, nor his primary source of income. He seemed to have half the government in his pocket and there was not a single man of influence in the capital that he could not have bought. In the light of my recent experience, and not wishing to fall foul of a second African administration within a matter of weeks, I elected for discretion as the better part of valour and turned a blind eye to our man's unorthodox business methods. After all, I did not possess a valid work permit for Ghana either.

By the time I went to Zimbabwe, although it may still have been Rhodesia then for it was definitely around the date of independence which happened in 1980, I had long ago shed my former persona of oil industry specialist. In fact I had passed through various specialities on my way to becoming a financial services expert, in which guise (or perhaps I should say *dis*guise) I was called upon yet again to head south to dispense the wisdom of great experience. In those days, before the wave of demutualisation, there were several hundred building societies in the United Kingdom, ranging from tiny local operations serving the needs of not much more than a single county town up to national organisations almost on a par with the banks. Quite a few of these societies were customers of ours, so we were well placed to supply proven systems to the two companies established on the same model of mutuality in Zimbabwe. I was despatched in response to their request for advice.

The role of the building society was very straight-forward, almost amounting to a type of social service: they lent money for house purchase in the form of a mortgage and they took interest-bearing deposits to fund those loans. That much I knew, but so did every UK citizen who had a mortgage, in other words practically every UK householder. Since that was virtually the full extent of my knowledge of their business, on my calculation I was one of roughly fifteen million people equally qualified to advise them. The strange thing was that in London we had dozens of real specialists who were *au fait* with every last detail of building societies' operations and their computerisation. The stranger thing was that the Zimbabwean companies, apparently run by indigenous whites, were happy to discuss their IT problems with me and to accept my advice, the nature of which is of no particular interest and in any case beyond my recall. But why? I may have been one-eyed, but they were certainly not blind.

During the period of my expertise in the financial markets I did not travel much abroad. One trip I do recall was to a bankers' conference in Monte Carlo. The idea, I suppose, was that I would meet lots of influential people and make contacts which might prove valuable in future dealings with the banks. This rather overlooked the fact that senior bankers were more interested in hobnobbing with other senior bankers than with some interloper from the computer world. As usual, however, those of like minds tended to gravitate together, so I found myself at one bar or another late into the night with a bunch of fellows who showed no inclination to discuss anything as seriously boring as banking. I even spent one evening with several South Africans at the casino, despite my aversion to gambling, a position I hold less on grounds of high moral principle than from fear of losing money. On this particular occasion we all chipped in equally to a kitty which we were prepared, and I think fully expecting, to lose. One of our number sat at the blackjack table while the rest of us stood in a semi-circle behind him telling him what moves to make. We none of us knew what we were doing, but it worked and when we decided to quit we were so flush with funds that the night's drinking still left us each with a handsome profit.

The keynote speaker on the last day of the conference was Marshall McLuhan, the Canadian philosopher I have also seen referred to as a communications scholar, which might be thought more likely to account for his invitation to address a conference of bankers. He was perhaps best known for giving the world such expressions as 'the global village' and 'the medium is the message'. I was lurking in the back row and after his talk he came and sat down beside me and we chatted throughout the following proceedings. Although I can't remember the detail of our conversation I do recall that he was an interesting, pleasant and modest man with a very original turn of mind. I felt lucky to have met him. Within a year he had died, at the relatively young age of sixty-eight or sixty-nine.

On leaving Rhodesia/Zimbabwe I continued south to Johannesburg, which did not impress me much as a city, being large, sprawling, ugly and full of unfriendly and resentful people. This should have come as no surprise, since South Africa was still subject to apartheid, a term that may literally translate as segregation or separate development but which in effect just meant the suppression of the huge black majority by the small white minority. Walking out after dark from my hotel in the centre of town I did not really feel safe and soon turned back. I was glad to be off to Cape Town after a few days, though sorry I couldn't spare the time to make the journey overland by train because I am told by those who have done it that the country is spectacularly beautiful and there is much to see on the way, including diamond mining and the extensive wine-producing areas.

The company had a sizeable business in South Africa and one of their most important customers was a UK-based bank, which had equipment of ours installed worth tens of millions of pounds. It represented for us a major strategic account in the banking industry worldwide. Its loss would have dealt a devastating blow to our reputation and our presence in the market, yet, despite the resources we poured in, we seemed always to be fighting some rearguard action, teetering on the brink of disaster. The purpose of my visit was to discover the reasons behind this string of crises and to make recommendations for remedial measures. The customer received me politely and spoke frankly of their concerns; our local management bent my ear painfully on all the problems besetting them, most of which were naturally outside their control and largely the result of the neglectful policies of the parent company, of which I was the convenient whipping-boy. The whole situation was in fact well understood by the company in London because the director of our international division sat on the board of the South African subsidiary and I am sure this troubled account was discussed ad nauseam at monthly board meetings. I realised I was unlikely to be able to tell him anything he didn't already know: thus, in addition to intelligence gathering, my role was one of reassurance that their difficulties were being taken seriously. So I wore my responsibilities lightly and spent as much time as possible enjoying the delights of Cape Town, which were manifold.

At a distance of twenty or thirty years (I returned for a second visit a few years later) my overall sense of Cape Town, nestling at the foot of Table Mountain, is one of whiteness. I am not referring here to the colour of the people but to the brilliance of the light on the whitewashed buildings. In my mind's eye I have a picture of an almost Mediterranean city lapped by an equally blue sea. That image, like so many others viewed dimly through the distorting mirror of time, may be a trifle misleading, but the truth, as one poet said, is how I remember it and if you remember it differently then that is your truth and who is to say the one is more truthful than the other. By the same token I see palm trees rustled by the breeze off the water, bustling cafés and bars full of large beer-drinking men towering over their tanned athletic-looking girls, and seafood restaurants displaying today's catch fresh from the shorefront market.

One day I borrowed an old Volkswagen from our provincial manager and set out for the Cape of Good Hope, the mountainous promontory some twenty five or thirty miles south of Cape Town, rounded for the first time, as far as anybody knows, by Vasco da Gama in 1497, though it beats me how anyone can possibly know. In my ignorance I had thought I was going to the southernmost tip of Africa, but a glance at the map shows that from Cape Town the coast runs south east for about a hundred miles or so to a point some fifty miles further south than the Cape itself. Heading back to town in the late afternoon I had gone no distance at all when there was a loud crack and the car shuddered to a halt. All my efforts to restart it, including such advanced techniques as swearing and turning the key repeatedly in the ignition, failed to stir it to life, so for a modest fee I recruited a couple of sturdy chaps who happened to walk past and together we manoeuvred it off the road, where I left it lying half on the verge and half in the shallow ditch which ran alongside. It was an old banger, but it wasn't *my* old banger, so I felt guilty at leaving it at the roadside, though there was no obvious alternative: I would just have to face the music. I now had to make my way to the nearest railway station, which turned out to be a few miles to the north and which, I'm guessing, may have been Simonstown. Wherever it was I walked there, arriving very hot, sweaty and a bit bedraggled. I went straight to the window and requested a second class ticket to Cape Town. 'Sorry, sir, that won't be possible' said the railway clerk, which slightly threw me. 'Why is that?' I asked, innocently but in retrospect rather stupidly. Seeing my puzzlement he obviously judged me a newcomer to the system and explained: 'As a white man you are not allowed to travel other than first class. Second class is for blacks.' It must have pained him to utter those words, being a black man himself. For the second time in the space of an hour or so I was left with a distinct feeling of guilt.

In the office the following day I explained what had happened and apologised for abandoning the car. The owner was philosophical and didn't blame me at all. He rang a garage and asked them to send someone to have a look at it, emphasising that it might be on its last legs so they shouldn't waste too much time on it. I'm sure they didn't. Word quickly came back that the rear axle was broken and it wasn't worth repairing. No mention was made as to whether the car had already been cannibalised, but I suspected if not then it very shortly would be.

I could think of places I knew where it would have been picked clean within hours, leaving only a carcass. As for the railway, about a dozen years would pass before the law would allow blacks to travel first class and, presumably, whites to opt for second, though whether that happens in practice even today I rather doubt.

Several years later I made another trip to South Africa. The intervening period was, I hoped, long enough either for people to have moved on or to have forgotten my first visit because this time I bore little resemblance to the erstwhile finance markets specialist, having adopted a new persona as an expert in an entirely unrelated field. On this occasion I gave a series of talks to audiences, mostly customers, in all the major towns. In addition to Johannesburg and Cape Town, to which my earlier visit had been limited, I went to Port Elizabeth, Durban and the capital, Pretoria, each of which has its own distinct character. Unfortunately for the most part I was obliged by my fixed schedule to fly from one engagement to the next, so there was still very little opportunity to explore the countryside in between. The exception was a weekend which I spent with a colleague and his wife at a vast game reserve a few hours drive to the east of Johannesburg. For those who may think that a game reserve is a highly controlled environment where semi-domesticated animals live contained lives under the permanent gaze of a stream of tourists, I would point out that there is nothing of the zoo about it at all. The one we visited covered hundreds of square miles, with all the great beasts of the jungle, and many lesser ones, free to lead a normal existence in their natural habitats. We were lucky enough to come across a fair number of them during our weekend break, while avoiding too close an acquaintance. By and large the animals showed a total disregard for our car, though if they had realised that it contained defenceless, warm-blooded creatures their attitude might, I suppose, have been different.

There was a curious aspect to this second visit to South Africa. Shortly before I was due to leave London I was present at a rare family gathering and at one stage in conversation with my elder brother Jeffrey.

'What are you up to these days?' he enquired, as one does.

'Not a lot,' I replied unhelpfully, then added, 'I'm going abroad in a couple of weeks. It'll be nice to get away from this awful weather for a while.'

'Where are you off to?'

'South Africa. I'm doing a tour of some of the main cities, addressing groups of people who will probably only be there out of politeness or duty and for the free drinks afterwards. With luck, though, we'll have a bit of fun. We usually do.' (In the event my audiences were uniformly attentive, most friendly and keen to linger and chat over a few drinks, so we did indeed have some fun.)

'Well, you won't believe this, but Judy and I are also going to South Africa at about the same time. What are your dates?'

I told him when I was leaving for Johannesburg and that I would be there initially for several days. Our dates apparently coincided exactly.

'Where will you be staying in Jo'burg?'

'I shall be at the Sandton Hotel,' I said.

'So shall we.'

When we parted that evening we were still marvelling at the incredible coincidence. What might be the odds against such a happening?

'Cheerio. See you at the Sandton,' we said.

But there was a further twist in the tale. At the hotel reception I left a note in Jeff's pigeon hole telling him when I was likely to be around. On my return I found another note saying sorry we missed each other, but how about such-and-such a time? This pattern was repeated once or twice and eventually we both moved on, without managing to find a mutually convenient moment to meet or bumping into each other in the lift. We were six thousand miles away from home and staying literally yards apart, but the nearest we came to making contact was an exchange of scribbled messages on hotel notepaper.

Shot For A Lunchbox

Just weeks after the premature death of my father and about a month before my thirty-fourth birthday I was posted to Jamaica on a one year contract. I was not too happy with this arrangement because I felt that twelve months was barely time to get my feet under the table, but there was a reason for it. The company had a policy of appointing local people to manage our subsidiaries overseas. This was an altogether sensible approach, which we managed to make a hash of time after time, and we'd done it again here. The internal candidate we had lined up for the job decided, with some justification, that the company was dragging its heels and he wasn't prepared to wait any longer, so when he was offered the position of computer manager with one of our customers he didn't hesitate in accepting.

One of my objectives was therefore to woo this man back to take over from me as general manager at the end of my year. Unfortunately for us he was quite content with his new position, in which he was earning more than we were prepared to pay him, so he made it clear that he was no longer available. For some time he proved a slightly awkward customer, in the literal sense, bearing a grudge against the company for raising his hopes, if not actually promising him the position of general manager, and then failing to deliver. The result of all this was that I stayed for almost two years, then handed over to another expatriate Englishman, at which point we seemed no nearer to implementing our policy of so-called localisation. Whether we ever appointed a Jamaican to the top job, and if so when, I have no idea.

My successor and his wife arrived on the island and we took them to dinner at the Liguanea Club, where I was, and no doubt he would become, a member. Sitting at a table on the terrace he bombarded me with questions about the country, the city of Kingston, the politics, the people and the way of life. He wanted to talk about the business as well, but I insisted that this was a social occasion and work could wait until we were in the office the next day. It was obvious that he had read a certain amount about Jamaica and seemed even to have some preformed views. Eventually he touched on the issue of personal security in a town which, he had heard, was bedevilled by violence, gun crime and general lawlessness. Was it, he asked, a safe place to live?

I could easily have shrugged this question off with the standard advice not to believe everything you read in the newspapers, but frankly I had not taken much to this chap so my response was a bit mischievous, an oblique reference not designed to improve his peace of mind. I opened that day's copy of *The Gleaner*, the best Jamaican daily broadsheet, turned to page eight and pointed him to a short report, not much more than one column inch, buried at the bottom of the page.

'Mr Carlton Ledward', it read, 'was shot dead by an unknown assailant as he left home for work yesterday morning. The motive is believed to have been theft. The victim's lunchbox was stolen. His widow said it had

121

contained a bacon bap and a banana. The police are pursuing their enquiries'.

I may not have explained to him that this happened in a very poor area of West Kingston slums, the most deprived part of the capital, and that he was unlikely to be gunned down as he left the Sheraton Hotel to take a taxi to the office, whether or not he was clutching his lunchbox. Neither do I remember if I mentioned the evening when, after all the staff had left, I stood at the office window and watched a rather comical exchange of fire between the police and some so-called bandits on the Old Hope Road. It might have been far from comical had they engaged each other at closer quarters, but I knew that the probability of a hit on a moving target using handguns at a range in excess of thirty yards was always low. So, I imagine, did the police, who showed an understandable reluctance to close further on their quarry and, with more discretion than valour (though it may have been the other way round when they filed their report back at the station), accepted an honourable draw and retired to their vehicle to go in search of a quieter life and less demonstrative villains.

The only other time I was anywhere near gunfire in Jamaica I was within earshot but not near enough to be in danger. For a part of my tour we lived in the hills above Kingston and about half a mile up the lane was a training hotel where young cooks, waiters and reception staff went to learn their trade. One night there was a break-in and shots were fired, though the incident did not last long and it was never clear if there were any casualties. Our next door neighbours were a British police adviser and his wife, a charming couple, neither of whom ever said a word about his role with the local force and, even if he was *au fait* with all the details, his lips were sealed on this occasion too. Instances of gun crime and murder were indeed common in Jamaica, or more precisely in Kingston, but they were mostly confined to disputes between gangs or individuals in the poorest areas of the town. This does not make them any less serious, nor the victims any less deserving of sympathy; it is simply to point out the relative rarity of violent crime affecting the middle classes and in particular the expatriate community. By and large, if you were sensible you were safe.

In some cases being sensible meant taking precautions. During our first few months we lived in a townhouse on the outskirts of Kingston. It was a small, two storey, two bedroom affair in the middle of a terrace of almost identical houses, replicated on two other sides of a rectangle, in the centre of which was a communal garden and swimming pool. There were advantages and disadvantages: the house was not exactly spacious and there were limits to privacy; on the other hand the garden was a very pleasant haven, with its fruit trees including bananas and three varieties of mango, the pool was a great convenience and the whole arrangement was ideal for children. But for many the major factor was that it was a secure compound, bounded by a high wall and patrolled by an armed guard, though I don't think he was required to use his weapon while we were there.

Before too long we tired of the constraints of living in the townhouse. We moved to a much larger single storey house that I could never bring myself to call a bungalow, though on the strict definition of the term that was what it was; to me, bungalow always suggests seaside and, if not flimsy, then insubstantial. This was none of those things. It was a solid, smart house in an affluent suburb, surrounded by enough land to justify the part-time employment of a gardener, approached up a steeply sloping drive and through an impressive pair of wrought iron gates. It seemed to lack little except a swimming pool. In reality it came with a great deal more than we had bargained for: rats. Not just your average inoffensive rats, but huge voracious vermin as big as a small cat and not harmlessly running around the garden but in the house, raiding the kitchen and scurrying noisily along the exposed beams in the living room and bedrooms. There was a large spreading tree that slightly overhung the roof and my theory was that these were tree rats, though that view was never authoritatively confirmed, nor indeed that any such species existed. We called in the experts in pest control, on the assumption that this was a euphemism for extermination. They shook their heads, sucked their teeth, tut-tutted and declared this to be the worst such case they had encountered. Even as they put down industrial strength poison they made it clear that they could not guarantee success and, as if fearing a further invasion while they were on the premises, departed in a hurry, leaving us a supply of the allegedly lethal red grain for the delectation of our uninvited guests.

At the first signs of the problem we had notified our landlord, an apparently prosperous Jamaican businessman. On the telephone he expressed astonishment that we should make what he obviously took to be an accusation of deceit on his part. When, at our request, he paid us a visit, he denied that there had ever been rats in the past and refused to accept the evidence of the current infestation, namely the dirty traces marking their regular passage on the beams and along the skirting boards in all the rooms. He was thoroughly unsympathetic.

The efficacy of the poison was proved when one day we discovered a monster specimen stretched out dead on a bedside table but, as you can imagine, our reaction was more one of horror than of satisfaction or relief. Perhaps it was the exception to the rule because none of the rest seemed to succumb, at least not in public, and there were plenty of further sightings.

Early on in this miserable saga we had taken to sleeping elsewhere. Fortunately I had retained the town-house we had previously occupied in order to accommodate a salesman who, with wife but no children, was shortly due out from England for a two year tour. Since he had not yet arrived, the house was available, so every evening we would carry the sleeping Freddy to the car and transfer ourselves for the night. We still held out some hope that the rats would be eliminated and that it would be possible to remain for the full term of our lease. When the situation failed to improve I found alternative accommodation for us and advised the landlord that I was terminating our agreement forthwith.

His response was to threaten me with the courts, to which I said 'Carry on. My company will contest any action.' On receipt of my reply to his solicitor's letter the lawyers must have advised him against proceeding, probably on the grounds that he had a weak case, since not only was the evidence scampering around for all to see, but it was abundantly clear that the presence of rats was nothing new in that house. They would also have pointed out that he had little to gain and a reputation to lose, although if the latter was true it was not one that had come to my notice.

So we abandoned the rat-house to its fate and literally headed for the hills. If we had had a lucky escape, we now experienced an even kinder spin of the wheel of fortune. It was my secretary, a generous and thoughtful person, who came to the rescue. She had a sister who was married to a well-to-do German businessman. They had been living in Jamaica but had just recently decided to move to Fort Lauderdale in Florida, where I gathered he had an interest in commercial property. Their house in the hills above Kingston was unoccupied but still fully furnished and ready to move into; they were more than happy for us to move into it during their absence, which at that stage was indefinite and might well be permanent. It was a sort of upside down house which tumbled down the hillside from the entrance under a carport at the highest point to a terrace giving onto the garden. This was equally divided between lawn and swimming pool, with flower borders and two banana trees. The lack of a mango tree was hardly felt since our neighbours' garden was well stocked and we were welcome to as much of this luscious fruit as we wanted.

Our new home was off Stony Hill Lane, about six miles due north out of town, at well over a thousand feet and with terrific views over Kingston which, as I have observed elsewhere, looks better from a distance. We were not really isolated but neither were our neighbours very close at hand so, largely for reasons of security, though in the event it also proved good company, we acquired a dog, a medium-sized mongrel which had been mistreated by its previous owners but which rapidly recognised its good fortune in being transferred to a friendlier family. For about a week every morning when I left for the office the dog would chase after the car until it gave up some five hundred yards down the lane and slunk disappointedly back to the house, where it would doze for most of the day on the terrace. It was nothing like your typical guard dog, a snarling Alsatian say, and it was difficult to think of it as an effective deterrent. But appearances can be deceptive: this one instinctively understood its role and carried it out intelligently. Whenever I arrived home at a late hour or if I had reason to get up in the middle of the night, the dog would invariably be wide awake, sitting alert in a commanding position on the flat roof of the kitchen, ready to bark its little head off to warn of the danger of any would-be intruder. Such was its concentration on the job in hand that it would ignore me completely.

Jamaica is a stunningly beautiful island, whether it is the thickly wooded Blue Mountains that dominate the capital and which really do have a bluish hue in a certain evening light, or the quaint little towns and villages in the hills of the interior, poor but proud, or the traditional old fishing ports or the superb beaches in the secluded coves of the north and west coasts. Yet, in a sense, Kingston lets it down. There is little of beauty here, with its straggling avenues winding to nowhere in particular or from one suburb to the next and not much of a focal point, no heart from which the arteries of the town might radiate, no shape. True, there is some pattern to the downtown area near the harbour, which by day is the main business quarter and at night becomes a poorly lit maze of narrow streets that for safety's sake are best avoided. You might expect that there would be some elegant colonial architecture surviving from the Spanish past or from the more recent era of British influence, but if so you would be disappointed. There are compensations, principally in the gifts of nature such as trees and flowers. To see whole streets ablaze with the brilliant scarlet of the tropical poinsettia and banks of bougainvillea is unforgettable.

Apparently the city of Kingston was the accidental by-product of a disaster. In 1692 an earthquake destroyed the island's foremost trading post of Port Royal, whereupon the surviving merchants decamped to set up shop in a small community across the harbour which in time grew to become Jamaica's capital, but that was not until 1870. Before then the capital had been Spanish Town, now much smaller than Kingston, inland and barely fifteen miles away to the west. The population of Kingston in the early 1970s was roughly three hundred thousand, making it the largest city in the English-speaking islands of the Caribbean and home to about one sixth of all Jamaican inhabitants, though there are of course many more of their countrymen living elsewhere, notably in the UK and Canada, whether temporarily or permanently.

A mere matter of weeks before my arrival we had moved our offices from the downtown business quarter to a modern, purpose-built facility on the Old Hope Road in New Kingston. I'm unsure whether we were trend-setters or followers but from the standpoint of most interested parties our new base was much more conveniently situated. We occupied the upper and half the lower floors of a squat two-storey building, the rest of which served as the surgery and administrative offices of a general medical practitioner, a Chinese Jamaican named Dr Wong, which is the Cantonese equivalent of Smith. Whether the surgery or the office was the more important focus for the doctor was a moot point, since he was as much businessman as medical man, if indeed the two roles could be separated at all. Dr Wong was sometimes charming, more often irascible, with a short fuse, a pretty wife, a broad Jamaican accent (hilarious to the ears of somebody accustomed to the sound of the

Hong Kong Chinese) and a voice that was frequently raised in some angry altercation with a patient or client and was clearly audible on the floor above. Apart from being our family doctor, he was also the owner of the building and thus the company's landlord, from which you can gather that it was a fiendishly complicated relationship. I only managed to avoid unpleasantness between us by delegating everything to do with premises to my financial controller, who happily was quite capable of standing up for herself and could shout as loudly as Dr Wong. I suspect he never fully forgave me for declining to deal with him direct, feeling aggrieved at being obliged to conduct affairs, mostly concerning our complaints at various problems and deficiencies in the building, with the messenger.

Unfortunately we had plenty to complain about. The office was cheaply constructed, badly designed and the layout was difficult to modify. There were constant teething troubles, with the electrics, the air conditioning, the cloakroom or the toilet facilities regularly malfunctioning, not all of which, to be fair to the doctor, were necessarily his fault. My room, in the centre of the building, had no window and thus no natural light, and one lady programmer quickly came to me with the bitter complaint that she had worked loyally for the company for seven years only to end up sitting at a desk in the corridor. A young man applied to us for a job, was interviewed and considered to have good potential, but he turned us down in favour of one of our competitors whose superior premises must have left him in no doubt where his interests would be best looked after. This was a blessing in disguise as we were saved the cost of training him. In no time at all he was opening the bowling for Jamaica and the West Indies and went on to a very distinguished test career as possibly the fastest bowler in cricketing history. Now in his middle fifties, Michael Holding is a seasoned commentator and a trenchant critic of the West Indies cricket establishment whose squabbling and lack of strategic vision has, in his view, contributed so much to the current parlous state of the game in the Caribbean.

There was another game going on which came to consume a disproportionate amount of my time and energy, driving me almost to distraction. We had an unusual customer whose business was off-shore data preparation: companies in the United States sent quantities of documents, the contents of which were transcribed onto magnetic discs that were then returned for processing on those companies' own computers. The rationale for these seemingly complicated operations was, of course, that data preparation was labour-intensive and labour costs in Jamaica were a fraction of those in the USA, so even allowing for flights and profit margins it was still well worth it. In short, our customer was little better than a sweatshop, a large roomful of poorly paid girls working round the clock in shifts to meet tight contractual deadlines for turn-round. Unfortunately this also demanded a high level of equipment reliability, which we signally failed to provide. With the benefit of hindsight (wonderful thing, hindsight, except that it always comes just too late to help) we should never have sold these machines in a place like Jamaica. It was far too risky: we didn't manufacture them ourselves but bought in the entire systems and consequently lacked detailed engineering expertise. They were continually breaking down. We allocated our best account manager and our most experienced engineers were dedicated full-time to the installation. We brought out specialists from the

UK at great expense. They would fix things and declare themselves satisfied that the systems were in good order and that the fault would not recur. The moment they set foot on the plane taking them home, some new disaster would strike and we were back to square one. Nobody really had a clue what to do because there seemed no end to the catalogue of faults, whether a recurrence of known weaknesses or new problems that popped up to mock our conscientious but exasperated engineers.

This company was owned and run by two improbable partners, both Americans. One was a rather smooth, educated business type named Mort, who lived in the States and whose role it was to sell the company's services and negotiate contracts, including prices, standards of quality and the crucial issue of deadlines, which invariably carried financial penalties for late delivery. His partner was his opposite. Big, burly, rough-hewn, a Jewish ex-prizefighter from Brooklyn whose language was as colourful as his background would suggest, he put me in mind of the actor Lee J Cobb, who featured as the bad guy in a number of westerns and played the thuggish reactionary juryman in Twelve Angry Men. He was responsible for the production end of the business. His wife, a Chinese Jamaican, was the hands-on supervisor of the machine room and underneath a mild exterior was as tough as old boots.

Irwin seemed always to be on the verge of violence. He kicked out two of my salesmen and banned my engineering manager from his premises because he wore his hair shoulder length. His promises of future action were largely unrepeatable here, but he regularly threatened to hurl our equipment into the street, a threat I felt him perfectly capable of carrying out in a moment of uncontrollable fury. He announced that he would deal with nobody at the company except the general manager, that is, me. He appeared to have two objectives in life: the first was to make money, which he did by meeting his customers' contractual deadlines whenever our rotten, malfunctioning systems permitted; the second, for the reasons outlined above, was to make my life a thorough misery, an aim in which he was largely successful, by laying siege to my office, by issuing an endless stream of strident demands, by unrelenting verbal abuse and by his refusal to pay our bills. In the circumstances I might have felt a bit sorry for myself, but I had a great deal more genuine sympathy for him than he could have realised. We were both in an impossible situation.

The nearest we came to a partial ceasefire was at the pub. I don't recall how it started, but after a while Irwin took to ringing me to suggest a beer on our way home in the evening and it became a habit several times a week. I didn't look forward to it but it was a means of holding the line: somehow we could be more honest with each other on neutral territory with a glass in hand. We would meet at a bar called the West Indies, referred to as the Windies. There we would have a few bottles of Red Stripe, the local brew, before switching to something stronger. At that point we would also move round to the back room, which was full of gambling machines of the one-armed bandit type. I have never liked gambling but this was what Irwin wanted to do, so I went along with it on the principle that the customer is always right, even out of hours. It was a surreal and paradoxical situation in which we found ourselves: the unsatisfactory supplier and the highly dissatisfied customer constantly crossing swords by day, while regularly clinking glasses by night. War and peace. The storm before the calm.

*

It was my good fortune, however, to have available the perfect escape from this disagreeable environment. The Cayman Islands were far less well known as a tax haven (or more accurately a no-tax haven) in those days than they are now, though in the early 1970s there were already something like one hundred and seventy banks with offices on Grand Cayman. Of course they were not really offices, merely addresses of convenience. Even so, they required the usual accounting services, which in their case were provided by an enterprising firm that set up on the island for just that purpose. This firm installed one of our computers and with an engineer of ours permanently on-site it was a very satisfied customer. It was also a reason, or rather an excuse, for me briefly to abandon the strains of life in Kingston and to relax in a place where stress was a foreign concept.

Grand Cayman, though tiny, is by far the largest of a group of three islands and lies in the Caribbean about two hundred and fifty miles north-west of Kingston and roughly the same distance due south of Havana, capital of Cuba. It is odd that they are described as a group since the other two, the minuscule Cayman Brac and the even smaller Little Cayman are eighty miles away to the east. They are a British Overseas Territory, which as I understand it means that the Queen is Head of State, there is a Governor who I imagine is an appointed Caymanian and a government headed by a Prime Minister.

Two other key characteristics that underline the Britishness of the place are that English is the official language and they drive on the left. This didn't count for much when, as I was told by a resident, the only two cars on Cayman Brac were involved in a head-on collision on the only stretch of road on the island (there was neither need nor room for a second). When

133

Columbus first discovered the islands in 1503 he named them Las Tortugas because they were swarming with sea turtles. Getting on for a century later Sir Francis Drake landed there and decided they should be known as the Cayman Islands after the *caiman*, a type of small alligator, so in the tussle for recognition between these two relatively low forms of life, the alligator came out top dog. All of which may be a bit confusing. Anyway, for nearly three hundred years the Caymans were lumped together with Jamaica as a single British colony until Jamaica's independence in 1962 when they acquired their present status.

The number of businesses registered in the Caymans is said to be greater than the population, which in 2006 was estimated to be in excess of fifty thousand. This figure is astonishing given that the number of people living on Grand Cayman in the 1970s was probably nearer five thousand than ten. You could drive through George Town, the capital then as now, without realising you had done so; it was more village than town and the splendid Seven Mile Beach boasted two or three hotels at most. The islanders were literally all known to one another and found nothing remarkable in the fact that nobody locked the front door when leaving the house to go about the business of daily life. After all, there was no crime and little to exercise the almost non-existent police force, if you ignore the occasional fracas outside a bar when more than the usual quantity of rum had been consumed. If the population estimate is roughly correct and you double it to cover the ceaseless invasion of tourists that fuels the local economy, there can hardly be standing room on the island these days. What a contrast with the situation nearly forty years ago, when we had Seven Mile Beach more or less to ourselves. And what a blessed relief that was from the stresses and strains of life in Kingston, to which we had all too soon to return.

Wherever we lived in Jamaica we were not very far from Constant Spring Golf Club, which I joined as soon as I arrived on the island and where I played every Saturday morning. If it was not the most attractive course it was a pretty fair test and certainly the most charmingly named. I used to play with various expatriate friends: a Canadian engineer employed by one of the utilities companies, whose wife, obliged to kick her heels at home while her husband was at work and her children at school, had taken increasingly to the bottle and was becoming something of an embarrassment; an Australian academic who was a better golfer than I was (not difficult), a moderate drinker, physically fit and, in the mould of the majority of his compatriots, always fiercely competitive; and a Lancastrian who gave a running commentary on his game, his every remark reassuring himself, and me, that if only he had done something slightly different he would have hit a cracking shot. So, for example, 'If I'd just taken an easy five instead of smashing that seven iron' or 'if I'd aimed off a bit for the wind' or 'if I'd given myself more time over that putt' and he would habitually round off by saying, 'Oh well, if my aunt had balls, she'd be my uncle'.

Awaiting my arrival outside the locker room each Saturday was Peter, my caddie. At least, Peter was how he first introduced himself to me at the start of our partnership and what possible reason could I have for questioning the coincidence? It was some time before I discovered that he frequently caddied for a friend of mine on Sundays and on these occasions his alias was changed to Bob. My friend Bob was surprised to learn that on Saturdays his faithful caddie was working for me under a pseudonym. Peter/Bob was a likeable, bright lad of about fourteen, who I trust spent the other five days of the week at school, otherwise he was certainly heading for a serious crisis of identity. In addition to his role as bag-carrier, he had a couple of other endearing characteristics. The first was his propensity to give technical advice. This mostly concerned the art of putting, and usually came in the form of an exhortation not to leave my putt short. I wondered if Bob had the same problem. 'Doant shart it, sah' he would say, and was often disappointed. His other skill was rather more devious, but deployed to my considerable advantage. I was driving the ball fairly straight but he obviously decided I could do with a bit more length, so as he arrived at my ball he would, without noticeably breaking his stride, pick it up between his big toe and its neighbour (he wore no shoes, perhaps for this very purpose) and march forward a further ten paces or so down the fairway before releasing it. When I caught him up he would congratulate me on another good drive. I eventually spotted what he was doing and told him that this was cheating and he should stop it. This brought a sly smile to his face, an acknowledgement that he had been found out, but also the merest suggestion that he had only been doing his job, which was to help me to win and perhaps to help himself to a larger fee as a consequence.

After a few months I also started to play tennis once a week, which I thoroughly enjoyed. I was leaving the Liguanea Club one evening, walking to my car, when I passed a couple in tennis gear. There was nothing unusual in this and I didn't pay them much notice, but seconds later the fellow turned and called my name. I went back and was surprised to find it was an old friend from Hong Kong, an Australian who batted number five for my team, the HKCC Optimists. Like me, he didn't have the time to play cricket in Jamaica but was a pretty good tennis player and from then on we arranged to play each other one evening a week on the grass courts of the Liguanea Club, while his wife teamed up with some of the other lady players. Because he was a better player than I was, my game improved greatly over the next few months, to the point where I managed to win the odd set and even, on rare occasions, the best of three. Malcolm Shearer had been a contemporary at school in Adelaide with Ian Chappell, who captained Australia on their tour of the West Indies that year. When the team arrived in Jamaica he and his wife threw a party for the tourists and I was also invited. It was a very lively and enjoyable evening, during which I was introduced to the Australian captain, who had a reputation for playing it hard on the field but who proved a charming and drily humorous man off it. To my surprise he expressed interest in the league cricket Malcolm and I had played in Hong Kong and was quite happy to talk shop, even to discuss the challenge he and his colleagues faced with the West Indies' fast bowling attack, not that he needed any advice from me on the subject.

One way and another I managed to escape from Jamaica often enough to break up the routine and regularly recharge batteries with a welcome change of scene. The company had an operation in Trinidad, some twelve hundred miles south-east of Jamaica, just off the coast of Venezuela. This is roughly the distance between London and Palermo in Sicily, though because both are in the Caribbean the general view from England was that they were next door neighbours. Slightly further from Jamaica and a short hop of a couple of hundred miles or so to the north-east of Trinidad lies the much smaller Barbados, the most easterly of the Caribbean islands and a part of the Windward group. We decided to have a mini sales conference in its capital Bridgetown. That is what we called it but in reality it was no more than an excuse for a jolly. Barbados is by no means the smallest of the Caribbean islands despite being barely twenty five miles long and fifteen at its widest point. Everything there is to see can be seen comfortably in a day, if not in an afternoon. Nonetheless, it is well worth exploring as it is a lovely place, very rural, relaxed and relaxing. Life seemed not to be taken too seriously and most Barbadians (Bajans) in my brief experience had a smile on their faces most of the time. Perhaps this had something to do with one of the main planks of their economy, rum, the other being tourism, which is greatly assisted by smiles all round. You felt they deserved to succeed. Although, since 1966, Barbados has been an independent state within the Commonwealth, it has a total population of around a quarter of a million, making it considerably smaller than, for instance, the English town of Leicester. Apart from sugar and its alcoholic by-product, this tiny island has produced a phenomenal number of the world's great cricketers over the last century.

For our three day meeting we chose a hotel at Bridgetown which was not only on the beach but boasted its own pier, where we hired a small conference room. This was something of an extravagance, given that our little gathering was never intended to justify the status of a proper 'conference'. But it did prove useful as a launch-pad for extracurricular activities. After a leisurely breakfast on the terrace we would repair to our workroom in casual dress, or rather undress, meaning swimming trunks, to discuss and agree the programme for the day, before plunging into the warm blue sea directly from our own private balcony. By the time we had taken a gentle swim and dried ourselves in the sun there was maybe an hour left for a presentation and discussion of some work-related topic before thoughts turned to lunch and the afternoon's entertainment. The evenings after dinner were spent diligently sampling the island's principal source of export revenue.

Island-hopping in the English speaking Caribbean, unless you were fortunate enough to own a boat and have plenty of time on your hands, was normally undertaken by means of BWIA, standing for British West Indian Airlines. They ran a fleet of small aircraft, most of which seemed at any one time to be grounded for reasons of maintenance or repair, resulting in frequent delays and changes of timetable. The longest flights from Kingston to, say, Port of Spain in Trinidad, would take upwards of five hours with a couple of stops, including the US island of Puerto Rico. The trip to Barbados took at least four hours. BWIA thus had a slightly dubious reputation as a carrier, which gave rise to a variety of jokey alternative acronyms such as But Will It Arrive?, leading to the rather more contrived Better Wait In Airport.

I should add that BWIA delivered me safely to Bridgetown and back with no alarms, though for the return trip I must have been very effectively anaesthetised.

When my father died in July 1972 mother was aged sixty-six. A year later she came out to visit us by banana boat, which in the circumstances I thought both adventurous and brave. I can't remember the reasons for the decision to travel by sea: they may have been economic, or it may have been a disinclination to fly, though she had a few years earlier flown to East Africa without complaint. Perhaps I suggested it as a means of extending her holiday and as an interesting experience in its own right. Whatever the case, it was not a particularly large vessel, and certainly not a thing of beauty, but she enjoyed the journey and the company of a small group of fellow passengers, and came through the odd rough passage without succumbing to anything worse than a mild queasiness. She must have felt quite excited as they put in to harbour at Port Antonio in the north-east of the island and she spotted us waiting on the quayside.

Mother's presence provided me with the perfect excuse to duck out of my regular sessions with Irwin at the Windies pub, though of course it did nothing to ease the problems he continued to cause me in the office. During the day Cristina entertained her, taking her to the shops, to lunch or on little sightseeing outings before picking up Freddy from school and perhaps resting in the garden or having a dip in the pool. We also spent a week at a hotel on the north coast, where Freddy had to be rescued from a raft that was caught by a swift current and was suddenly heading for Cuba at an alarming rate of knots. By then I had taught him to swim in the pool at home but hundreds of yards back to shore was a different matter.

Anyway, when the time came to take mother back to board the boat – the same one – at Port Antonio for the return journey, she was looking tanned, healthy and all the better for her Jamaican holiday. She had undoubtedly enjoyed her stay, but I never really knew what she thought of the life we led or the people amongst whom we led it.

*

Soon after mother's visit I was summoned, along with my colleagues from all over the world (except those running our subsidiaries in Europe, which belonged to a separate division) to an international division management conference in Cairo. Why Cairo, you might reasonably wonder: was this the new hub of the technological future? Was the Nile valley about to become the silicon valley of the Middle East, shifting the balance of power in electronics from the eastern Pacific to the eastern Mediterranean? (For that matter, had the term 'silicon valley' even been invented in the early 1970s? I doubt it.) Well, no. The reason was actually rather more pragmatic. We had long had a successful company in Egypt, racking up good profits year after year. The trouble was that we had not been allowed to repatriate these surpluses and there was limited scope for sensible reinvestment in that market, so the cash was piling up in the bank to no particular purpose, save in the hope that some day the strict Egyptian currency controls might be eased and it could all be shipped back to London. Some hope. It was therefore decided that a meeting in Cairo could be held at no real cost at all, apart from the fares to fly everybody in. Which of course represented a very considerable cost, given that they converged from Australia, New Zealand, the Far East, South, East and West Africa, the Caribbean, USA and Canada.

I had to travel via London so Cristina and Freddy came with me for a holiday in England seeing family and friends. We stayed a few days at a hotel in Kensington and on a Saturday morning went shopping, together with half the rest of the world, on the High Street. There, in a moment of careless inattention, we managed to lose, or at least become separated from, Freddy, who had just had his seventh birthday.

For a minute or two we were stunned into indecision as to whether to stay where we were and hope that he reappeared or to search for him down the street in the direction we had been going, assuming that he had simply wandered ahead. I started walking at a fair clip, as quickly as the crowds of shoppers would allow, stopping briefly to peer into any shop that I felt might have tempted him in, and with a mounting sense of doom.

Reaching the end of the High Street, now in a state of desperation, I came upon the Commonwealth Institute and there, sitting swinging his legs on the low wall separating pavement and lawn, was an entirely unperturbed seven year old greeting me as if nothing untoward had happened. 'Hi, where have you been?'

The Cairo conference was a strange affair, remarkable for the volume of alcohol consumed, albeit that Egypt is ninety percent Muslim, and for a major row with our director. The event was based on a series of presentations by territory managers, from which pertinent points were taken as subjects for general discussion. Thus widely applicable lessons could be drawn from individual experience. The opening session hit the buffers at the very first mention of the word problem. Our director interrupted the speaker to issue an angry rebuke to him and a warning to us all. The word problem carried a negative connotation that was unacceptable. He would not tolerate the defeatist attitude signified by the use of such a word; we in international division did not have problems, only opportunities. Some opportunities might present us with challenges, which would be tackled positively.

The reaction to this outburst came close to uproar. The speaker responded that, yes, he had plenty of opportunities and was not short of challenges, but it was pointless and absurd to deny that in some areas there were problems, which could usually be defined as matters beyond his immediate control, to be resolved in other parts of the company. It was for this very reason that he was raising them in this meeting, where others might have similar concerns or might have constructive solutions to suggest.

There was vociferous support for this view and it quickly became clear that the director, although in a minority of one, was not prepared to concede or compromise. At this point there was an intervention by the managing director of our Australian subsidiary, the second most senior person present, who proposed a break in proceedings to allow tempers to cool. During this adjournment he took the director aside and suggested that if he didn't modify his stance he would have a rebellion on his hands.

'These are not a bunch of school children,' he insisted, 'they are all senior managers and it is inappropriate and insulting to lecture them on how to frame their presentations.'

His wise counsel was heeded, at least to the extent that the director adopted a less confrontational approach, and the conference was able to continue in a calmer, more measured atmosphere. Naturally nothing was said as to what exactly had passed between the two during the break, but at the close of the event I flew back to London via Athens, where I had several hours to kill before my connecting flight, as did our Australian MD for his, so we went for a couple of beers to a bar where he told me the whole story. I have related this episode at some length because I thought it interesting in itself, but it was also, to my mind, an early example of a sort of political correctness, long before that term had been coined. Worse still, our director had, in a sense, cast himself in the Orwellian (Kafkaesque?) role of the thought police.

Outside of the conference room there was much revelry, at dinner and late into the night, as is often the way of these things. As regards matters cultural, I fear most of us failed to take full advantage of the opportunities. Yes, we had a look at some of the old parts of Cairo and paid a dutiful visit to the pyramids, though this was more in the nature of a drive past than a thorough tour of inspection. There was also a special evening in a typical Bedouin tent out in the desert, where we ate a typical Bedouin dinner consisting of such delicacies as goats' testicles and sheep's eyes and drank the fine wines so redolent of the nomadic Arab life. Of course this so-called tent was to the average camel driver's shelter what Buckingham Palace is to a Victorian terraced two-up two-down in Brixton. During our feast we were introduced to the subtle and exotic arts of the belly dance, as performed by a local beauty of indeterminate age, who, perhaps assisted by the quantities of Bordeaux with which we had washed down our sheep's eyes, charmed us all to bits with her anatomical acrobatics. As an international management team we bonded furiously together, while one or two, in their cups, tried vainly to bond with the belly dancer. Then we all went back to our mundane lives in Jamaica, Johannesburg and elsewhere, having delivered a short, sharp boost to the Egyptian economy and leaving behind us a bewildered local management and a much depleted company bank account.

As I write this, the programme of recovery and return to some sort of normality of life is still in its early stages in Haiti, which was devastated by a massive earthquake a couple of months ago. Its capital, Port-au-Prince, was virtually destroyed, causing the deaths of citizens numbered in hundreds of thousands (will anyone ever know exactly how many?), mostly buried in the rubble of fallen buildings which were never designed to withstand a shock of this magnitude. It is difficult to comprehend the scale of the disaster and terrible to contemplate the fact that it should be visited on one of the poorest nations on earth, a nation so poverty-stricken that you might suppose it had nothing further to lose. Yet what little it did have has been lost.

This dark corner of the earth has, over the decades and centuries of its history, suffered more than its share of human misery and disaster, but for the most part this has been man-made if not always self-inflicted. Populated almost entirely by African slaves, Haiti became a Spanish colony after its original discovery by Columbus, then passed into French hands around the turn of the eighteenth century. A hundred years later French rule was overturned following a slave insurrection led by the improbably named Toussaint L'Ouverture. Since then the country has never enjoyed political or social stability, its course being scarred by civil strife, military coups and counter-coups, assassinations and the violence of successive brutal dictatorships entailing the terrorisation of ordinary people by their secret police. When, from time to time, elections have been held, they have been marred by irregularities, corruption and violence, contested by the losers and have never led to lasting democratic government. The USA, seeing Haiti as in their back yard and a potential source of danger to the stability of the region, has twice sent in troops to establish or restore a fragile order.

Haiti occupies the western part, about a third, of the island of Hispaniola, the other two thirds of which is the Dominican Republic, whose capital is Santo Domingo. It is a mountainous territory largely covered with forest, the areas available for agriculture being limited to the few fertile valleys. It supports, or rather fails to support adequately, a population of some six million, most of whom are illiterate and live in dire poverty. Ethnically the people are ninety-five percent black and five percent of mixed race, the so-called mulattoes, between which groups there was much tension and hostility in past times. The country is overwhelmingly Christian, perhaps four fifths Roman Catholic, with the great majority also practising the cult of voodoo, which is characterised by sorcery, spirit possession and the magical religious elements derived from the African superstitions of the former slaves.

Cuba and Haiti are geographically Jamaica's closest neighbours, each a little over a hundred miles away at the nearest point, though Kingston to Havana is about five hundred miles as against the three hundred to Port-au-Prince. In political terms, however, neither was a particular ally and Cuba's doors were firmly shut to the non-Communist world, including tourists, so we went for a long weekend to Haiti.

At the time of our visit the country had just emerged from fourteen years of ruthless repression under the dictator president Doctor François Duvalier (1957-71), known as Papa Doc, who had deployed the notoriously thuggish secret police, the Tontons Macoute, to do his dirty work for him, suppress any political opposition and maintain him in absolute power. On second thoughts the word 'emerged', however, is inappropriate here, since the presidency had passed immediately, dynastically, to his son Jean Claude, thenceforward to be known as Baby Doc, who continued the same repressive regime, ruling for even longer (1971-86) before eventually being kicked out and accepted into exile in France. This gesture of welcome, or at least of tolerance, is something of which the country in which I now live should be thoroughly ashamed. Duvalier *père et fils* were both evil monsters who deserved to be arraigned and punished for their crimes against their own people rather than granted asylum in a civilised European country. Baby Doc was firmly established in power by the time of our visit and there was a noticeably edgy feeling to the whole place.

As you might imagine very few tourists were tempted to make the trip to Port-au-Prince, and of those who did only a tiny minority was white, so we tended to stand out. The principal effects of this were twofold: first, although prices in general were low, we were charged significantly more than locals were for the same item, but of course in most cases they couldn't afford even the lower price; secondly, we were the constant target of people who wished to offer their services as unofficial guides or were simply reduced to begging. For those who have nothing except the rags on their backs it is understandable, but nonetheless poses an uncomfortable dilemma for the privileged visitor. Where do you draw the line? Do you put a coin in every outstretched palm or do you smile, shake your head and pass on, hoping that whatever you spend may make some ultimate contribution in the form of increased employment?

The streets of the city were poorly maintained, dirty, noisy, and chaotic, despite the paucity of vehicles other than taxis and the odd overcrowded bus. The buildings were almost uniformly run down, with the exception of the presidential palace, which was extremely grand, in a good state of repair and freshly whitewashed and painted. It was also surrounded by high security fencing and heavily guarded by the president's élite military corps. It said everything that was needed about the dictator's lifestyle in the midst of the abject poverty of his people. He rarely left the safety of the palace and never without an armed motorcade surrounding his bullet-proof presidential limousine. The few tourist hotels, as opposed to those that were no better than doss-houses or brothels, were kept in rather smarter condition than their neighbours on the main streets, but still wore a slightly dilapidated air. Many houses bore, to the imaginative eye, the traces of a quaint, even a pretty past, with facades decorated in ornate fashion, little towers and balconies now badly deteriorated but once finely carved, all in the fretwork style sometimes referred to as gingerbread and reminiscent of the old French quarter of New Orleans. The whole place was on its uppers, broke.

By pure coincidence, just before going to Port-au-Prince I had been reading Graham Greene's novel *The Comedians*, which is of course set in Haiti, so I was looking forward to visiting some of the places that formed the backdrop to his story, and possibly enjoying the vicarious pleasure of tracing a little of the lives of his characters. (I think it was coincidence, but it is possible that I read the book for background because we had already decided to go to Haiti, or even that we went as a result of my reading it.)

The Port-au-Prince described by Greene was real enough, unsurprisingly perhaps since he had written it barely a half dozen years earlier, and at least some of the locations were more factual than imagined. For example, we had no difficulty finding Brown's *Hôtel Trianon*, naturally not its real name, where the body of Dr Philipot, Secretary for Social Welfare (a good joke, that), was discovered at the deep end of the empty swimming pool and Marcel, Brown's mother's Haitian lover, hung himself from the chandelier of the bedroom in which she had just expired. No great powers of observation were needed to pick out officers of the Tontons Macoute, often resembling Greene's sinister Captain Concasseur, an arrogant and menacing presence behind his permanent dark sunglasses, his pistol ever ready for the casual curtailment of life, more like a Chicago mafia boss than a member of the state secret police. We went one evening to the casino at which Brown caught the eye of Martha, the young German wife of a fat Ambassador from some unspecified tinpot South American republic, with whom he immediately embarked on a rather bored affair. Having no appetite for gambling I risked nothing at the tables, but I closed my eyes and pictured the scene of their meeting, the Ambassador's wife following Brown's every turn at the board, her faint smile signifying more than merely satisfaction at the success of her copycat betting. She had made the first move, while her husband sat at her side, watching but seeing nothing. Or seeing everything but choosing to do nothing, having his own reasons for letting his wife's affair take its course unimpeded.

So our long weekend in Port-au-Prince was a mixture of reality and make-believe, the grinding poverty surrounding the occasional oasis of relative prosperity, the shadowy menace of the Tontons Macoute, the fascination of the architecture and the early evening rum punch on the verandah of the 'Hôtel Trianon'.

Looking out of the window as we flew back to

Kingston I was alarmed to find how low we were, and not just low but slow, seeming to hover like a glider above the glistening water off the endless sandy beach that stretched into the far distance. For a few moments I was convinced that we were going to ditch in the shallows, before suddenly, with a last effort, we cleared the airport perimeter fence and drifted gently to a halt on a runway shimmering in the heat of the Jamaican afternoon.

When I tell you that pretty soon we took off again for another holiday break, you will begin to suspect, if you have not already concluded, that my two years of Jamaican residence were mostly spent anywhere but in Jamaica. This would be understandable from the emphasis of much of this chapter, but it would be wrong. A quick mental calculation suggests a total of days absent from the island of about twenty-five, and certainly no more than thirty, which works out at less than five percent. My absences were for the most part on business or work-related. So that's alright then. We can go off to Mexico with a clear conscience.

We flew to Mexico City via Miami, where we stayed overnight in a depressingly grubby hotel in what is referred to as downtown, which seemed to us to have no redeeming features. I assume we were only there because there were no direct flights from Kingston, or perhaps because there were none that suited our timetable. I can't recall why we chose to visit Mexico City in the first place and I retain only the haziest of memories of what we found when we got there. We stayed in a part of the city known as the *zona rosa*, a term that may have reflected the pinkish tint of the stone used in the buildings in that quarter, though it may have had some entirely different derivation. It was a pleasant area of broad avenues, dotted with hotels, restaurants, cafés and bars, obviously favoured by foreign visitors, and a stark contrast to much of the rest of the city, which was densely built, overcrowded, poor and rundown.

We walked a lot, usually without any particular destination in mind, just absorbing the atmosphere. I think we ate and drank well, washing down the spicy food with quantities of cheap beer and wine as the fancy took us rather than at standard mealtimes. We went to a pelota match, the first I had seen, though Cristina, being half Spanish and having lived for a year or two in Spain, may have been more familiar with the game. I believe there are several versions, but the one we watched was played on a court with one long side wall and two shorter walls at either end. The principle must be a little like squash. Two players wear basket-like rackets attached to, as opposed to held in, the hand. From this cupped racket the small ball is hurled at astonishing speeds against the walls and the rebound is caught momentarily, before being relaunched with great accuracy into the angle of the walls to deceive the opponent. The pace of the ball, allied to the way the players could disguise the precise direction of the shot by subtle variations of timing, meant that at times we found it hard to follow and a point might be won or lost without our quite knowing how or why. The crowd was almost as fascinating as the match, being highly partisan and excitable. It was fun.

Mexico City is one of the most populous cities in the world (13.6 million in 1990). It lies in a bowl surrounded by hills and this geographical position makes it notoriously prone to heavy pollution, though I suspect things were not nearly as bad forty years ago as they have become with the growth in population and the increase in industrial activity. A journalist friend of mine, after thirty years of life in Fleet Street casting his beady eye on world events through the bottom of a glass at El Vino's and other such scribblers' haunts, was despatched to run his paper's bureau in Mexico City, the objective being in theory to encourage him to dry out, rather than to broaden his journalistic experience. Given that he also had a habit of about sixty cigarettes a day, this struck me as one of the most idiotically misguided decisions any commercial organisation could possibly take in the alleged interests of a staff member. Here he was, virtually alcoholic and a long term nicotine addict, so they sent him to a paradise of cheap booze in one of the most environmentally polluted cities on the planet.

Back in Kingston life and the pursuit of happiness were carried on much as ever, that is, with a deal of frustration and limited success. My salesmen energetically chased orders that rarely materialised; technical staff diligently supported customers who sometimes, they felt, took them for granted; maintenance engineers worked their occasional magic, knowing the next problem was just round the corner. The wars of the sweatshop continued unabated, punctuated by the resumption of ceasefire sessions at the Windies; Dr Wong flew off the handle no less regularly, crossing swords with my financial controller at the slightest provocation, at decibel levels that kept everyone in the neighbourhood fully informed of his outraged sensibilities. I still played tennis weekly, sometimes weakly, with my Aussie friend Malcolm, celebrating my rare victories with an extended spell at the Liguanea Club bar, in the company of regulars who could talk a good game but didn't bother with the actual playing; Peter the caddie never let me down on a

Saturday morning and frequently buoyed me up with his unorthodox strategies for improving my game, while on Sunday slipping chameleon-like into his alter ego role as Bob. In short, nothing had changed.

As the day of my departure approached I started to reflect on Jamaica and my feelings about it. Clichéd though it is, the most appropriate term to describe them must be 'mixed'. I am not alone in the view that Jamaica is one of the most beautiful places on God's earth. Some would go on to say, rather as many English do about France and the French, 'pity about the people', but I would disagree in both cases. Jamaicans cover the spectrum from friendly, cheerful and good-humoured to morose and mildly hostile to outsiders. It seemed to me pretty much like anywhere else in that the friendlier you were towards them, the more they were inclined to respond in kind. I found many, particularly among the older generation, to have a genuine charm, while the educated young sometimes gave the impression of impatience with the old order, a desire to have done with all vestiges of the colonial past, traces of which perhaps they still perceived in the number of senior positions, albeit largely confined to the private sector, occupied by expatriates like me.

The Jamaican economy used to depend on exports of sugar and bananas, from which it was barely able to scratch a living and a very hard one at that. Now the country earns its income from tourism. This is all very well, except that it changes the face of the landscape and affects the character of the resident population. Even when I was there the north coast was beginning to be developed to attract, accommodate and entertain the increasing numbers of Americans who wished to escape their winter for two weeks of sun and sand on an exotic tropical island. But of course the more tourists there are, the less exotic it becomes. However well designed, a hotel built in a lovely, unspoiled cove makes that cove less natural and less beautiful. Another hotel appears with all its attendant services and before long you have a resort, and in this sense a resort is an artificial contrivance, existing purely for the convenience of the unadventurous, who really feel more comfortable among their own. So the American holiday-maker spends his two weeks with fellow Americans in a resort that is less and less typical of the local environment, background and culture, which is itself a victim of its own success in attracting them in the first place. Meanwhile, as happens everywhere in the world when tourism comes to dominate the national or local economy, the people tend to become more and more cynical and exploitative, less sincere, putting on a sort of performance in caricature for the benefit of visitors who cannot, or choose not to, see the patent falseness of it all.

Despite these not particularly original observations, I have extremely pleasant memories of several parts of the island. The Blue Mountains rise spectacularly to well over six thousand feet and form a magnificent backdrop to Kingston. Beyond them are further ranges, reaching almost to the sea on the east and north-east coasts where there are, or were, a number of unspoiled villages and the sleepy little town of Port Antonio, which was a special favourite, partly because of its tranquillity, its traditional architectural qualities, its old-fashioned harbour and its lack of overt tourism. Among the beachside hotels in the vicinity were one or two of the most discreet and expensive in the Caribbean. At the other end of the island, to the west of the well-known and busy resort town of Montego Bay, you found the calm of Lucea and then at the most westerly point the seemingly undiscovered delights of Negril, whose wonderful beachfront was as yet undefiled by the developer's hand. What price now a quiet picnic on an unpopulated stretch of sand, free of the intrusive noise and bustle of the holiday resort that Negril must surely have long ago become? And in the gentle hills of the centre west of Jamaica there was the small country town of Mandeville, still resonant of old England, with its grey stone parish church overlooking the green.

In a guidebook entitled *This is Jamaica*, interesting and helpful when it was published some forty years ago, the author Philip Sherlock wrote a paragraph under the heading Driving in Jamaica, which you might think to be much like driving anywhere else. But no. He observed that:

In many countries it is good manners not to blow the horn save in an emergency. In Jamaica it is often good manners to blow the horn, not in an angry peremptory manner but as a way of saying 'Good Morning' or of warning pedestrians that you are approaching. This is not sheer Jamaican perversity. In warm countries roads are used for much more than travelling from one place to another. The road reflects the life of the country. It is a place for living, a place for conversation, for meetings, for trading. After sundown it may become a place of worship for white robed revivalists or a platform for politicians. It is a stage where salutations are shouted long before one comes face to face with one's friend, where news is given about an aunt in London or a husband in New York, where

small boys play a game of cricket or football,
where dogs go to sleep on the warm asphalt and
an occasional cow or donkey sets off on a sight-
seeing trip. Those things being so, it is proper
to warn pedestrians of your approach. Sound
the horn also when overtaking. The driver in
front may have forgotten to look through his
rear mirror or he may be watching the drama
of the road.

I am happy to give best to Dr Sherlock, himself a distinguished Jamaican, though I wonder if he was not
slightly overegging the pudding, tempted to romanticise
a trifle, particularly where the streets of Kingston were
concerned. It is true that in many tropical countries the
road can reflect the life of the country, but I never myself
spotted a white robed revivalist or for that matter a
politician in full spate, either before or after sundown.
There were certainly a lot of hooting drivers, some with
impatience, others issuing a warning that they had no
intention of slowing down, and many just hailing their
passing mates. Driving tended to be a rather casual
activity: it was a common sight to see a driver, even a
taxi driver, one hand on the wheel, the other draped out
of the window clutching a bottle of Red Stripe beer from
which he would take the occasional leisurely swig.

There was sometimes an equally casual attitude to
such impediments to the free flow of vehicles as traffic
lights. One of my expatriate staff needed some repairs to
his car, so his usual garage sent a mechanic to pick it up
at the office. Whether the work was ever done I know
not, but that evening the mechanic borrowed the car for
his own purposes, namely to drive home. Unfortunately
he met misadventure. Passing heedless and at speed

through a traffic light showing red he was hit square amidships by a bus travelling equally fast through the green light on the cross road. The distressing news of the accident was received the following morning: the car had been completely written off, but far worse, immeasurably worse, so had the poor mechanic.

Other tales involving cars and the motorist in Jamaica could strike a lighter note and some were not really about driving at all. Giving me advice, on my arrival in the country, about the different parts of Kingston, a friend suggested that if he was ever foolish enough to drive through Trenchtown, a district in the west of the city, and had the misfortune to suffer simultaneous punctures in all four tyres, he would in no circumstances stop but would instead accelerate. This had nothing to do with the car, of course, and everything to do with his personal safety in an area, whatever Dr Sherlock might say, where hostility to the stranger might be rather unpleasantly expressed. This is, after all, where the hapless workman with lunchbox met a sudden end; if a bap and a banana was sufficient motive, how much more so a decent saloon car, tyres or no tyres.

Kingston Airport is about half an hour from the new town, situated five miles along The Palisadoes, a narrow tongue of land running east-west, at points barely wider than the road itself, separating the Caribbean Sea to the south from the almost enclosed harbour on the other side. A chap driving to the airport to meet an incoming flight had the rotten luck of a puncture on his way along The Palisadoes. He pulled over to the shoulder and proceeded to jack the car up to change the front nearside wheel. Before he had made much progress another car drew to a halt behind him, the driver of which got out, went to his boot and calmly emerged with his own box of tools. Placing his jack at the rear he immediately set about removing a wheel.

'Hey,' exclaimed the owner, 'what the hell do you think you're doing?'

'Come, man, fair's fair. You take the front ones and I'll take the back ones.'

How's that for a demonstration of the old adage that there is honour among thieves?

We flew out of Jamaica for the last time, with no such mishap on our way to the airport, leaving behind us its distinctive tropical air, slightly sickly sweet, the scent of its glorious flowering trees and the sights and sounds of the life of its streets, the rasp of car horns in places overlaid with the insistent thumping rhythms of Bob Marley and his reggae band booming from strategically positioned loudspeakers, the better to distract the motorist even further. We were also leaving an island where, apart from the fast bowlers on the field of cricket, very little moved at more than a snail's pace, a characteristic that to some spelt charm, to others frustration. I had experienced both in good measure.

On our way home our first port of call was Orlando in Florida, near which is Disneyworld, the vast amusement park, creation of Walt and younger sister of the original Disneyland built in California (where else?) in the 1950s. Freddy had been looking forward to this for months; it was his treat. Disney parks are parallel worlds in which children can lose themselves in their fantasies, surrounded by all the outsized animal characters with whom they are familiar from the cartoon films they have seen and the picture books they have read. Yet there seemed to be more adults than children, equally moved to childlike wonder at the array of attractions, physically enormous people munching on their king-size burgers as they queued patiently for the next thrilling ride, ghostly underground mystery tour or possibly their next burger. It was my first brush with obesity and it was not a pretty sight. That said, it was difficult not to be impressed by the sheer scale of the undertaking and by the engineering ingenuity that had gone into creating this alternative fantasy world. And yet it quickly palled. Despite the slick presentation, there was after a while a depressing sameness, a vacuousness that could not be disguised by all the jollying along, all the false bonhomie. My heart sank at the prospect of a second day, but that was what had been planned and that was what we did. I vowed to myself never to enter another theme park in my life, a promise I have certainly kept. But Freddy was seven years old and loved every wide-eyed minute of it, so any distaste I felt was irrelevant; in the larger scheme of things it was all worth while.

The following day we bade farewell to Florida and touched down with some relief in Toronto, where we stayed with old friends for a week or so, winding down gently in town and country before our return to England and a resumption, for the moment, of life at home in Highgate.

Either Side Of The Curtain

It was never my good fortune to work in continental Europe, unless you count the period after my corporate business career (which at the time I didn't once think of as a career, more as a series of jobs) had come to an end. By then I had little need of a briefcase and if it accompanied me at all it would have contained no more than postcards, the odd hotel bill, a few restaurant cards, perhaps some official papers relating to plans for the modest development of our property in France, and a journal in which, for the only time in my life, I recorded my thoughts and the progress I was making in whatever endeavour was current. Whether or not this episode strictly qualifies for inclusion under the title of this book, it is here anyway, a couple of chapters down the line.

That is not to say that work, when it was not detaining me in distant parts, kept me permanently on the home side of the English Channel. In an effort to recall what I did and where I did it I have just cast my eye over the map of Europe and am surprised how many places I managed to visit, though I cannot always remember exactly the name of the town nor necessarily my purpose in going there. On the latter point there is often a certain mystery, the truth of which might be revealed if

I could only pinpoint the date and thus the particular expertise in which I was currently cloaked.

My first trip to France on business was to a refinery on the Mediterranean coast, probably somewhere near Toulon. For some reason they tend not to site ugly industrial installations such as refineries at St Tropez, Nice or Cannes. Of one thing I can be sure: I would have approached the task, whatever it was, with trepidation, conscious that my experience in the petroleum industry had merely skimmed the surface. Was there any subject on which I was qualified to advise them, other than what was being done on our computer at Llandarcy in South Wales? And if that was what interested them, why would they not get it straight from the horse's mouth? My old Welsh conspirator would have loved a trip to the south of France, would have revelled in the opportunity to fly his particular flag, never mind that his French might not have been entirely up to it. 'OK boys. Yer's what we're doin' in Wales, look you' might have had the French translator wondering whether he was up to it either.

Later I found myself occasionally in Paris where, as I have described in an earlier chapter, I was involved in nit-picking contract negotiations with a bunch of supranational bureaucrats planning a UNESCO-sponsored computer installation in Rangoon, Burma. They were not the sort of people who would hang around for a *demi* or two after work, let alone a night on the town, so my visits were rather quiet affairs. Later still, when I had assumed the guise of expert in the application of technology to the finance markets, I instigated and pursued discussions designed to lead to our marketing a state-of-the-art French cash dispenser, to bolster and complement our existing portfolio of specialist products aimed, so far with limited success, at the UK banks and building societies. This initiative scared the wits out of our ultraconservative commercial director, who eventually pulled the plug on the proposed collaboration, but not before I had established excellent relations with the French manufacturer and had some good times in Paris. (It is possible that he didn't really understand what a cash dispenser, or an Automated Teller Machine [ATM], was. Once I was in the office of a director of a large City investment bank who was also a non-executive director of my company, when he called his secretary and asked her to get him some cash before lunch not, as he confided candidly, because he couldn't spare the time himself, but because he didn't know how to operate the cash machine.)

My counterpart regularly took me out to lunch at some of the best restaurants in and around Paris, often Michelin starred. I had sometimes to remind myself that this was conventional enough, given that, unusually in this case, he was the seller and I was the buyer. I was more used to things being the other way round. He was also a keen golfer and invited me to play at St Cloud, where he was a member of perhaps the most exclusive golf club in the country. It is the sort of place where, after the game, sitting with a beer in the locker room, your golf shoes are whipped away by a flunkey the moment you take them off and they are returned cleaned and polished before you have emerged from the shower.

Unfortunately on the evening of our game the club dining room and bars had been reserved for a private function hosted by a member, an aristocratic chap called Giscard d'Estaing, who happened to be President of France at the time. So, rather like an artisan member of a posh English golf club (a category of membership now largely abolished as an anachronism, I am glad to say) I was able to experience only the locker room and the course itself, where I lost our match by a small margin to the better player.

For business reasons which are quite beyond recall, I once went on a brief visit to Spain and Portugal. Of Madrid I have no recollection at all, though I am now well acquainted with the city as a result of several stays with an old friend who has lived there for many years, and I like it very much. As for Lisbon, again I cannot for the life of me think why I was there, but I found the place poor, run down, charming and full of friendly people with whom communication was impossible beyond an exchange of smiles.

The Portuguese written language may have similarities with Spanish, but when spoken it sounded to my ear more as I imagined Russian to sound, guttural as I never expected a southern European language to be. Of course our local manager and his staff spoke adequate English, so that was no problem. I believe the Portuguese are our oldest allies and I definitely felt an ease in our relationship, whether real or imagined. That may have changed over the intervening years as Portugal has benefited massively from economic subsidies and support from the European Union, to which it is now utterly beholden, transforming large parts of the country for the better (as they would doubtless see it). On the other hand, spending a short holiday on the dramatically beautiful island of Madeira, a Portuguese territory, it was depressing to see that every available square foot of land on the south facing slopes in and around the capital Funchal was being built on. When I enquired why so many buildings were being started and then apparently abandoned with their walls just two or three feet above ground level, I was told that in order to qualify for EU funding they had to be under way by a certain date, which was now looming, so everyone was getting in while the going was good. The taxpayers in countries across Europe were thus forking out for the people of Madeira to change the face of the island in a way that will probably have a perverse effect on its ability to attract the tourism on which its economy depends. Such is progress, as seen through the blinkered eyes of the doctrinaire and remote European bureaucracy.

I remember slightly more of a trip I made to Holland, Denmark and Sweden in the company of a colleague based in London and responsible for some aspects of marketing support to our operations in mainland Europe. If I could also remember what those responsibilities were, it might give me a clue to the precise point of our tour, but alas, I have drawn another blank. At any rate we went to give a series of presentations to staff and customers, no doubt to enthuse the former and ingratiate ourselves with the latter.

Things went reasonably well in Amsterdam, or it may have been The Hague, or both. From my point of view matters became a little more complicated thereafter. The difficulty was that my luggage went missing on the leg between Amsterdam and Copenhagen. In normal circumstances this should not have posed an insuperable problem: after all, Danish men have to buy their clothes somewhere, even if styles may differ a little from Savile Row or Jermyn Street, not that I have ever felt the need to venture quite as far upmarket as that. No, it was a problem only because in those days the company failed to acknowledge, or were too mean to accept, that the fault was not mine and that they should at least contribute to the cost of replacement. I suppose they took the view that my suitcase was likely to turn up soon and in the meantime I should make do as best I could.

In the event it didn't catch me up until my return to London and I had neither the funds nor the willingness to re-equip myself at my own expense. The result of all this was that I borrowed my colleague's spare suit, which was most generous of him and would have been fine were it not for the fact that he was several sizes larger than me in every direction. So in Copenhagen and Stockholm I took self-consciously to the stage looking and feeling like Stan Laurel dressed in a suit belonging to his partner Oliver Hardy. I should be astonished if the misfit was not obvious to everyone in the audience, but of course they were far too polite to remark on it. We drowned our embarrassment at the bar in the evening, by when I had changed back into the casual clothes I had been wearing on the plane. Stockholm is a very attractive city, thanks to a judicious mix of the ancient, the traditional and the new, to the water that seems to surround it and especially the lovely unspoiled harbour. I contacted a Swedish friend who had a large airy apartment in an old quarter near the port. She was by then married to a successful musician, composer and conductor of one of Stockholm's principal orchestras. They were both free that evening so we all, including my company colleague, went out for a convivial dinner together after an aperitif at their flat.

On another occasion, in a different context, I visited a number of companies in Italy, Switzerland and Germany, technically all competitors of ours, in an attempt to procure, or in the first instance to identify, specialist banking products to fill the yawning gaps in our own product range. I took with me a member of my staff who was better qualified than me to make the necessary technical judgements and we seemed to be for ever hopping onto planes for the next short leg of our journey. This confirmed something I had vaguely been aware of before: whereas I had never managed to sleep on any of the many long-haul flights I had been obliged to undertake, on these and other short-haul hops I was quite unable to stay awake. Worse, I slept irresistibly in the cars which collected us from and delivered us back to the airport at each of our calls. Is there a word for this condition? Is it even a recognised condition? Anyway, it is little wonder that I hardly knew where we were at any given time, and I certainly don't know now.

The one place I do recall visiting was Ivrea, the home of Olivetti up in the mountains about fifty miles to the north of Turin. So much was it the home of this leading Italian manufacturer that it really should have been renamed Villa Olivetti, or some such, because the whole town revolved round the company's headquarters and factories, which provided employment for the great majority of its working inhabitants. Their head office had a rather unusual, not to say strange, feeling about it, both from outside and in its internal layout. This was explained by the fact, as we were soon told, that the building had been designed to resemble an Olivetti typewriter from the air. I'm not sure how wise that had been, given the rapid and radical changes in style brought about by technological advances, but on the other hand the old design did remain largely intact for several decades and now the building could be seen as a monument to the foundations of the company's continuing success. I found it also a rather endearing mark of eccentricity. So proud were the Olivetti management of their iconic architectural statement that they offered to take us up in a small company bi-plane to see for ourselves, but I declined, I hope with good grace, on the grounds that we had a heavy schedule and were a little pressed for time. It would have been nearer the truth to have admitted that I distrust small aeroplanes even more than I dislike big ones, and I certainly didn't fancy a low pass over Ivrea to pick out the detail of the beloved typewriter.

I suspect the rest of the trip was uneventful by comparison with Olivettiville, since to call my memory of it hazy would be to bring it into far too sharp a focus. Did we proceed to Zurich or was it Bern? And thence to Mannheim in Germany, or am I confusing it with Mülheim, in the more industrial region further to the north? If it seemed important at the time, in retrospect it could hardly be less so.

When I was at school the only two modern languages available were French and German, both of which I took at 'A' Level. Had there been further options such as Italian or Spanish, I think I would have chosen one of those in preference to German, and I'm sure I would have made greater use of it in my later life. With no opportunities to speak German, my knowledge withered on the vine and in any case French was always my stronger suit. Apart from the tour which I failed to describe in the last paragraph, there was just one occasion when I found myself in Germany for reasons associated with work. I was invited to give a talk at a conference taking place in Hamburg, a city to which I had not previously been. I forget the nature of the event and the subject of my own contribution, but I was determined to do better than simply stand and deliver my speech in English, though in fact that was precisely what was expected of me. Instead I put together two or three introductory paragraphs in German, which I read with a moderately convincing style and pronunciation, before declaring my talents exhausted and apologising for continuing in my own native tongue. This effort, my willingness to have a go, was roundly applauded (amazing, when you think that most of my audience of German businessmen could probably switch into competent English whenever the situation demanded) and whatever the quality of the rest of my presentation, it would be remembered, if at all, for the boldness of its introduction.

Mention of Brussels conjures up for many English people ridiculous European Union (EU) regulations on straight bananas or the banning from sale of misshapen tomatoes or the imposition of metric measures on a country that has for centuries been happy with its stones, pounds and ounces. (By the way, you can ask for a pound of carrots at any stall on a French market and that is what you will get. It is perfectly normal. On the other hand to talk in kilometres in England is absurd when all distances on the roads are measured and marked in miles and yards, though I am not sure whether the teaching of metric units in schools is a direct consequence of our membership of the EU or a function of a rigid curriculum centrally imposed by politicians too young to have been taught the old system.)

During the middle and late 1980s I paid fairly frequent visits to the temples of EU bureaucracy as Chairman of a European IT suppliers group part-sponsored by an EU department. We would meet in well-appointed conference rooms amongst lavish offices occupied by highly paid middle grade civil servants working on idealistic, and often fatuous, projects concerned with the promotion of pan-European technical standards in the IT industry. It was a fatuous exercise because, as we all know, the industry was no slouch in developing innovative ideas, and companies by and large preferred to back their own individual judgements in such matters. They didn't like being told what was good for them, and particularly not by people with no business experience. Seeing all this pointless activity and being aware of these civil servants' generous terms of employment at our expense, including accommodation and first class travel, was enough to make anyone eurosceptic. It all looked unnecessary, wasteful, like jobs for the boys. The same goes for the Commission itself, unelected politicians who, at least in the case of the British members, however elevated their earlier careers, have in some way failed at home: either forced through some indiscretion or misjudgement to resign from the government or to leave parliament or sacked as MPs by their constituency voters.

So the Brussels of the EU headquarters and all its bureaucratic overtones is never likely to be very popular with the British, but there is always the other Brussels, the old city surrounding the impressive and aptly named Grande Place, with its cobbled pedestrian streets full of lively cafés, bars and restaurants where you can probably eat in the traditional (French) style as well as anywhere in Europe. Burying our competitive differences, we certainly did our best to enjoy the restaurants of Brussels together, once the business of the day had been put behind us. And there is a wealth of cultural opportunities, art and music, not least the opera at the small but exquisite La Monnaie, where we went for a memorable night of Puccini with my elder brother

Jeffrey when he was working full time in Brussels. As is commonly the custom, that evening we left the theatre at the interval for a prearranged dinner at a restaurant just round the corner. I am sure, if you so wished, you could have your entrée before curtain up, your main course in the interval and your cheese, dessert and coffee after the performance. Very civilised.

A couple of odd coincidences happened to me during my trips to Brussels. The first was when I was on the interminable walk to board my flight at Heathrow, for some reason always at the far end of the terminal extension. Quite unexpectedly, since we saw each other rarely and neither knew anything of what the other was doing, I bumped into my younger brother Richard coming in the opposite direction. We had no time for more than the briefest of exchanges.

'What are you up to, then?' I asked.

'Just got back from Brussels,' he replied.

'What an amazing coincidence,' I said, 'that's where I'm going myself.'

'That's nothing. An hour ago I bumped into Jeff at Brussels airport.'

I wonder what the mathematical odds would be against such a series of encounters, though I doubt whether they could be calculated, given the infinite range of variables.

On the second occasion I was in Brussels for talks with our Belgian management. The purpose of the visit was achieved a little earlier than expected and I had a couple of hours to spare before my scheduled flight back to London. A friend of mine was working for an American company in Brussels, so I rang him to see if he could join me for a quick drink when he had finished work.

'Sure,' he said, 'I just need to finish something I'm

doing. Why don't you pick me up at my office. I'll tell you where to find me. Where are you at the moment?'

'I'm in our office here, with the MD, but I've no idea where this is in relation to you.'

'Right, that's easy. Turn right out of his office. Take the lift down one floor. Turn left out of the lift and mine is the fourth door on the left. Can you give me ten minutes, Peter?'

Not only was he half a minute away on the next floor down, but his office was directly below the one in which I was sitting. If I had raised my voice, I could probably have spoken to him without need of the telephone.

When the Berlin wall came crashing down in 1989 under the enthusiastic assault of Germans from both sides, the metaphorical iron curtain separating east and west Europe disappeared with it. The wall had been more than merely symbolic: it had been built not so much to keep westerners out as to imprison those to the east of it, and woe betide anyone attempting escape to the west, for if caught in the act they could expect to be summarily despatched by the guns of the east German guards. But of course access to eastern Europe was denied to most westerners, unless they had good reason for going, which excluded tourism, even had there been people keen to explore the delights of the laughably named German Democratic Republic and other repressive communist states. A certain amount of business continued to be conducted across the divide, including by my own company, and visits could in some circumstances be sanctioned by the issue of a visa. Not very long before the apocalyptic demolition of the wall and the collapse of the eastern bloc I was fortunate enough to be invited twice to countries which were then part of the Warsaw Pact and still living in the shadow of the USSR, but which are now both, broadly speaking, in the western camp as members of the European Union (though each asserts a fierce independence, not wishing to swap one foreign domination for another, however apparently benign).

On the first such occasion I travelled to Krakow in Poland, flying to Warsaw and being driven the two hundred miles, or thereabouts, south on rough roads through a flat and rather uninteresting landscape to the historic old capital, which lies on the river Vistula just to the north of the Carpathian mountains. Although we passed through two or three nondescript towns on our way down, we did not have the time, or perhaps the inclination, to stop, so I had my first real sight of a communist eastern European city when we reached Krakow. It may not have been a complete shock, since in the west we were schooled to expect a sort of grey uniformity as a defining mark of state communism. Yet it was precisely the drabness, the lack of colour and vibrancy, that was so striking. Initially, I couldn't quite put my finger on it. True, the streets were hardly buzzing with activity, every single building looked seriously in need of attention, if only a lick of paint, and there was a general air of neglect, of poverty even, the people as shabby as their surroundings. But there was something else. Then it clicked. There were no shops, or at least no shops as we would recognise them, that is to say no illuminated shop windows with goods clearly for sale and temptingly displayed. Nor were there any visible bars, cafés or restaurants, no sign of social life either advertised or spilling self-evidently onto the pavements and squares. As I later discovered, there was no shortage of pubs, but they were tucked well away, often hidden in basements, ill-lit establishments with no frills, serving an overwhelmingly male clientele with a choice of decent beer, rough vodka and cheap wine.

Astonishingly, Krakow emerged from the second world war physically almost unscathed. It is at its heart a mediaeval city that has somehow survived centuries of strife without serious loss or damage to the many fine public and private buildings that adorn its spacious squares and narrow winding streets. The central market square is particularly impressive, containing the ancient Cloth Hall and St Mary's Basilica, the massive Gothic church which probably outshines both the nearby fourteenth century cathedral and the slightly younger royal castle, historic home of the former kings of Poland. Nearly twenty-five years later I find it easy to imagine Krakow as a major tourist destination, promoting with justification its cultural heritage, its monuments, museums and art galleries, and boasting of its other side, its modernity and its youthful, lively open-air café scene.

All these impressions were gained in the short time I was there for the simple reason that I did not have a lot else to do. The purpose of my visit was to deliver a talk to a meeting of the Polish Computer Society, whose members were very welcoming and whose committee laid on a reception and a dinner that probably stretched their resources, and certainly my waistline, to the limit. I'm not sure how much of my speech was understood, but it was politely received and the principal means of communication with the President and his committee colleagues was the universal smile.

A few months later I went to Czechoslovakia, as it then was before it split into two independent states in 1993. I spent a couple of days in the beautiful city of Prague, sightseeing, being entertained by a charming young lady who was deputed to keep an eye on me and to act as my interpreter, and being briefed on our activities in the country and the event at which I was due to speak by our general manager, who, incongruously, turned out to be an Indian. How a man from Bombay washed up running an arm of a British business in Prague I never discovered, or if I did I have long forgotten.

I described Prague as beautiful and so it is, but from 1945 until 1989, when Russian hegemony over the eastern bloc countries effectively collapsed, it lived under Soviet domination. The severity of the communist economic regime ensured that Prague, despite its wealth of fine architecture, was poorly maintained and presented a dismal face to the world. The elegance of Wenceslas Square had allegedly been largely hidden behind scaffolding for the best part of a decade, although no work had been done. The story was that the labourers who erected the scaffolding immediately disappeared to better paid jobs in the black economy, but that seems to me to beg the question as to why they bothered to put it up in the first place. Just as I had found in Krakow, the everyday facilities of Prague – its shops, pubs, cafés, restaurants – were virtually out of sight. I walked for miles searching for life, peering into dim shops whose shelves were almost empty, wondering why everywhere was so dark and gloomy. Not only was it dark but it was dirty too, a consequence, it was said, of the universal use of coal for heating, which contributed to the high levels of air pollution.

Standing in Wenceslas Square and strolling through the centre of town it was easy to conjure up images of 1968 and the so-called Prague Spring, when a bid for a degree of independence and an attempt to establish a more liberal regime in Czechoslovakia was crushed as the tanks and troops of the Soviet Union and its satellites rolled in. I crossed the handsome Charles Bridge and had lunch in a restaurant high on the hill with fine views back over the river Vltava to the city and its prominent castles. One of these, Hradcany Castle, was the scene of what came to be known as the Defenestration of Prague (1618), in which Protestant nobles, reacting against the oppression of the ruling Catholic Habsburgs, hurled a number of their imperial representatives to their deaths from the castle windows. This apparently precipitated the Thirty Years War, which consumed Europe in an orgy of religious conflict that I cannot pretend to understand. Fortunately, life was a little more peaceful, if not exactly joyful, when I was there.

On day three of my visit we set out by car for the town of Prerov, several uncomfortable hours' drive to the east, where the conference I was due to address was to take place. We were held up on the outskirts of the town for about half an hour by a temporary military roadblock, while a huge convoy of heavy vehicles carrying Russian troops, weapons and equipment headed north towards the Polish border. When eventually we were able to proceed, we decided to check in to our hotel before meeting our hosts for dinner. The next thirty minutes or so alone made the whole trip worthwhile.

The hotel reception hall was a vast area of marble floor with no furniture and nothing to decorate the walls except matching photographs of the Soviet and Czech presidents. These two looked sternly down from their positions above a long bare counter to the right of the entrance. To all appearances the reception was unmanned, but as we approached a head slowly rose above the level of the counter to scrutinise us with the

175

utmost suspicion, as if to question our right to be there and our motives for invading her private territory. We were not fooled by the moustache and the five o'clock shadow: it was definitely a woman. I knew that from the spy films I had seen, in which every floor of every building in a communist country was kept under surveillance by an identikit caretaker who never budged from her stool at the end of the corridor. She was straight out of central casting, a strapping figure measuring about four feet by four feet. Perhaps she had been an international shot-putter. These were the days when eastern European women dominated the burlier athletics events and regularly mounted the winner's podium to sing along with their national anthem in a full-throated bass baritone. A cartoon in an English daily perfectly captured the then current doubts over the true gender of certain female Russian athletes. In a popular television programme called *Top of the Pops*, singers' performances were judged by a mock jury who held up cards marked either 'HIT' or 'MISS' to signify likely success or failure. The cartoon showed a muscular female in shorts and Olympic vest parading before a jury whose verdicts were equally split between 'MISS' and 'MISTER'. Anyway, the receptionist, if I may briefly dignify her with the title, grudgingly passed me my room key, which was in size and weight more like the key to a prison cell. I made my way to the sole lift in the far corner of this echoing hall feeling less like a welcome hotel guest than a condemned man facing a long spell of solitary confinement.

What greeted me when I turned the key to my door on the sixth floor was not at all what I expected. Opening off a spacious hall were three doors. Straight ahead was a large bedroom with adjoining bathroom – nothing remarkable there. To the right was first a small but comfortable sitting room, furnished with old leather armchairs in the 'club' style, a thick woven rug on the parquet floor and the walls lined with books, none of which was comprehensible to me. Next to it was a dining room, undoubtedly the *pièce de résistance*. Six elegant chairs were arranged round a handsome table laid with a row of three large lidded china serving dishes, with a solid oak sideboard along one wall. Against the end wall opposite the window there were two substantial glass-fronted dressers, one containing all the china that could possibly be required for a banquet for six people, the other packed with fine Czech glassware, including several sets of wine glasses and decanters of various sizes and designs. I wondered how long it had been since this room had been used for its true purpose. Was it conceivable that a modern hotel guest would invite his friends to join him for dinner and that the hotel would produce and serve a meal worthy of this extraordinary setting?

The answer to that must surely have been a negative. Like the reception area downstairs, the overall effect was mournfully sad. My rooms (for they were more than a suite but less than an apartment, lacking a kitchen) were kept clean, the furniture polished, the glass and china immaculate on their display shelves, but the whole assembly was frozen in some past time, as in a museum, a lifeless reminder of a more prosperous and flamboyant age. Perhaps it was in wry recognition of the pointlessness of all this former grandeur that I was charged the equivalent of three pounds sterling per night for my accommodation. Was that a day's wages for the ex-shot-putter, who had resumed her position, crouched soundless and invisible behind the reception counter, as I left the hotel?

By prior arrangement we met our hosts for dinner

at a restaurant, though it may have been some sort of members' club. It was certainly not somewhere you simply walked into from the street, if indeed such places even existed in Prerov. We made a furtive approach down an unlit alley and knocked on an unmarked door that was opened by someone who seemed to know that we were expected and duly let us in, albeit without any show of welcome. Three or four people awaited us at one of a number of round tables, several of which were occupied by groups drinking beer, as we were about to do. After a few rounds a waitress started to deliver food to our table and we switched from beer to red wine. By now I was so hungry I could have eaten a horse and for all I know I may well have done so. Course after course arrived, with little to differentiate them from each other. It was pretty heavy going: sausages and potatoes followed by a hunk of unidentifiable meat with boiled cabbage, more savoury dishes, and so on until I felt I was sinking like a ship holed below water, but never a hint of anything light or frivolous like a dessert. Somebody paid the bill, a trivial matter of a few worthless notes, and we crept out into the darkness of the town rather as we had arrived, back up the alley and, with relief, by foot through the deserted streets to the echoing silence of the hotel.

The following afternoon I was taken to the conference centre where I was to give a talk to a gathering of the Czechoslovakian Computer Society, a much bigger affair than the one I had attended in Krakow a few months earlier. On this occasion there was an audience of perhaps 120 to 150, mostly young people in their twenties and thirties, many of them graduates in mathematics and computer science from the country's best universities and employed as analysts and programmers, the majority with a reasonable command of English. I was shown onto the stage where there were about eight chairs behind a long table facing the hall. Seated here were the chairman, the society's president, secretary and three or four invited bigwigs, plus me as the guest of honour. I was introduced to each of them in turn on my way to my place beside the president. A short while after I had taken my seat I became aware that another person on the top table, a late arrival to whom I had not been introduced, was trying to catch my attention. This chap was tipping his seat and looking along at me behind the others' backs, smiling and making vague but unmistakable gestures of greeting. I smiled back politely, hoping not to show my embarrassment at being hailed in this way by a complete stranger.

At the end of my presentation I took questions from the floor and, after thanks from the chairman, the session was wound up and we all repaired to another room for drinks and informal chats. After a few minutes my conversation with some delegates was interrupted by the society's president. He had with him and wished to present to me the fellow who had been so keen to attract my attention on the top table. 'Mr Knight' he said, 'may I introduce you to Mr X, the president of the Polish Computer Society. But I think you are already acquainted.' I'm not sure I carried it off, my feigned attitude as of an old acquaintance happily renewed, but the truth is I wouldn't have known him from Adam, although he had been a very generous host to me not long before in Krakow.

Briefly Down Under

Towards the end of the 1980s I travelled, for the one and only time in my life so far, to Australia. Just before that, however, I had a rather strange experience in the USA. As a consequence of my involvement in an IT industry suppliers group promoting international standards in Europe, I was invited by one of the big American computer manufacturers, also represented in the group, to participate with them in a sort of trade fair in Boston. We were strong competitors, though admittedly not in the United States, where our pathetic presence in the market meant that we were not seen as a threat to anybody. The suggestion was that I might have informal conversations, in my capacity as chairman of this European group (thus conferring on me some sort of impartiality which I did not feel), with any of their customers who might be interested in the relevant developments in Europe. I would also give a couple of talks to their invited audiences.

This prospect was greeted by my directors with long faces and raised eyebrows. Nobody quite knew how to respond: fraternising with a major competitor had never been in the repertoire. Was this a unique opportunity or a complete non-starter? Was it perhaps a trap? Was I to be Daniel, thrown defenceless into the lions' den? I was myself in at least two minds and in both of them very nervous about accepting the invitation. But after much deliberation I decided it was worth the risk and the trip went ahead.

In the event, despite feeling something of a cuckoo in the nest, I enjoyed the week. It helped that I knew one or two of the competitor company's senior managers and got on well with them. I stayed in the pleasant town (well, Boston suburb really, though it does have a separate feel to it) of Cambridge, famous for Harvard University, founded in 1636 and the oldest in America, and the Massachusetts Institute of Technology (MIT), of more recent vintage but no less distinguished in its field. This felt like something of a home from home, living as I then did in the even better known university town of Cambridge in the English fens. I had ample free time to look at Boston, which I found attractive, and to sample its bars and restaurants, particularly those clustering round the old harbour. I have never had any wish to live in the United States, but if I did I would probably choose somewhere in New England.

One afternoon a Scots friend and I decided to escape for a game of golf. We went to play a public course, of which there are many all over the States, usually of a high standard of design and maintenance, as this one proved to be. The caddie master took our green fees and told us to join two other players who were making their way to the first tee. We introduced ourselves and set out as a four-ball match, Brits versus Yanks. One of the Americans was friendly, talkative and generally extrovert; the other seemed to be his opposite, a bit of an oddball, who said nothing at all until we reached the fourth tee. Then, before we drove, he made an announcement. 'This here's the dick-out hole' he told us, but we weren't sure we had heard him correctly and in any case his meaning was far from clear, so we asked for clarification. He repeated exactly what he had just said, as if he was reminding us of one of the rules of golf, and only when it was obvious that we hadn't understood did we get further explanation. 'See, the ladies' tee is quite a way in front of us. If anyone's drive finishes short of the ladies' tee, he has to play the rest of the hole with his dick out.' As I recall, that was his sole contribution to the conversation that afternoon. For the record, we all managed to remain properly dressed throughout the round.

Flying direct to Australia must be a hellish journey, taking, as it does, nearly twenty-four hours, and it's a wonder anyone survives it without at least suffering deep vein thrombosis (DVT), a dangerous condition to which I believe economy class passengers can be particularly susceptible, not because of their limited financial resources but as a result of their limited room for movement once they have taken their seats. I flew first to Hong Kong, but I don't recommend that either. A non-stop flight lasting fifteen hours is not my idea of fun, especially at a time when the company was having one of its frequent austerity drives and condemned all staff, regardless of status or mission, to travel economy. Not even the pretty, smiling Cathay Pacific hostesses could make it bearable. If you have to do it, don't try to work when you arrive. You feel like a wet rag and are about as useful. I limped through a couple of meetings but shouldn't have bothered.

It had been seventeen years since I left Hong Kong and there had been enormous change. My overwhelming feeling was not of nostalgia but of claustrophobia. My hotel room was on the thirtieth floor but there were plenty higher than that. Hong Kong is always on top of you (and doubtless a great deal more so now, almost another quarter of a century on), there is so little space as the sky-scrapers are pushed outwards and upwards and it seems impossible to escape the hordes of people scurrying purposefully hither and thither. True, it is spectacular; it exudes energy; it screams wealth; and yet you know you don't have far to go before you hit poverty. Money, large and small, probably changes hands faster here than anywhere on earth: it is a temple to Mammon.

I tried to track down old friends, but apparently they had all moved on. Eventually I found one and we met for a drink in the Mandarin, though it was not a great success. Apart from half-hearted reminiscing there was not much to say. He was serious, proper, formal even, an example of what I now remembered as slightly old-fashioned colonial manners. No chance, I thought after a few minutes, of him letting his hair down. He had made it to the top of his law firm and, still under fifty, he was shortly to retire with wife and family to Western Australia, where he could look forward to perhaps thirty odd years slowly wilting in the sun.

After three days in Hong Kong I was not unhappy to be on my way again, though hardly thrilled at the prospect of another long flight, the eight or ten hours down to Sydney. This was even more uncomfortable than the first leg of my journey. Half the passengers seemed to be moving to Australia lock, stock and barrel. I don't know what they had checked in to the hold, but they brought into the cabin with them everything but the kitchen sink, and a few seemed to have that with them too. Belongings that wouldn't fit into the overhead luggage lockers was stowed under seats and between legs, to the point where we were all virtually locked in our places. If we had avoided it on the last occasion, DVT would definitely get us this time.

My arrival in Sydney marked the start of a hectic schedule of meetings and conferences which saw me bouncing around the south-east corner of this vast country until I barely knew where I was at any particular time. As a consequence I brought back few worthwhile memories. Of course I saw the Sydney Harbour Bridge and the Opera House, but had no opportunity for a close look. I thought the city was impressive and I walked on Bondi beach, but it was out of season and a bit desolate. I discovered BYO restaurants, where they have no licence to serve alcohol, so you are invited to Bring Your Own: strange, in a country that produces so much wine and lager-style beer. But then, the licensing laws in Australia were hardly logical, with the so-called six o'clock swill followed by total drought until the next afternoon, by which time the six o'clock swillers were ready for another sprint to the finishing line.

Melbourne, the country's second largest city and for a brief period in the early twentieth century its capital, is said to be the most English of Australian towns. I imagine this reputation was based on its topography (a collection of villages?), its architecture and a population that included a majority of relatively recent migrants from the mother country. If so, I wonder whether it is still true today, since the relaxation of what were extremely tight rules on immigration have led to a new influx of non-anglophone Europeans and Asians of various nationalities. Anyway, I was there barely long enough to make the most superficial acquaintance with the place, before dashing back to Sydney, fulfilling an early evening engagement and flying off immediately to Tasmania, a lovely island, so they say, of which I remember virtually nothing. I could probably have said 'nothing at all', except that when I walked into the dining room of my hotel I recognised the first person I saw. He was not someone I knew personally, but a man widely known to the British public as a prominent leader of one of the biggest trade unions and as such very active in national politics. He was in the company of a good-looking lady considerably younger than himself and quite evidently, from their behaviour, not his wife. I was almost tempted to pass their table and offer a little aside to the effect that 'it's a small world, isn't it, and there's nowhere to hide, but don't worry, I'll keep it to myself'. I doubt that a proud local would be too impressed with my admission that this is my only real recollection of Tasmania. I was even uncertain as to which town I visited, but a glance at the map confirms that it was Hobart, not Launceston, because I was definitely by the sea.

Returning to the mainland, I had an early morning meeting in Brisbane on a Friday, following which I hired a car and set out for the weekend up the coast at a resort called Noosa Heads. Although I refer to it as a resort, it was not nearly as developed as that suggests nor as I am told it has since become, having more the feel of somewhere rather out of the way, uncrowded, relaxed, a pleasant backwater. At the time I had no idea that my cousin Janet, a couple of years my junior, lived there, as she does to this day.

In the mid-1990s I attended a lunch at my old rugby club in London, where I met several of my contemporaries, friends I had not seen for many years. One of them, then living in rural Gloucestershire, suggested that

I go down for a weekend, in a month or two when the weather should have improved, and we could have a game of golf at his club, Minchinhampton. A few weeks later I rang to check when he would be free and his enigmatic reply was:

'Oh dear, you're just too late, Pete.'

'How do you mean?' I asked.

'Well,' he said, 'we're emigrating to Australia on Friday.'

'Good Lord. That's a bit dramatic, Brian. Where exactly are you going?'

'We're going to Noosa. The plan is to find a house with a garden that has river frontage where I shall moor the boat I am going to buy. After that it'll all be plain sailing.'

'You seem to have everything well worked out,' I said, 'but what happens if there's nothing like that available on the market? I imagine they don't come two a penny.'

'I'll build one.' He spoke with complete confidence. 'You have to have a little project for your retirement, Pete.'

Some project, I thought. And the next thing that occurred to me was that, what with my cousin Janet and her husband and Brian and his wife and Elaine, a girl I knew in Hong Kong who has a house there, I must know a goodly proportion of the residents of Noosa, Queensland, Australia, and not long ago I had never heard of the place.

My return journey was via Singapore, where I stayed for three days, visiting the office a couple of times but otherwise just winding down after a hectic tour. Modern Singapore is an extraordinary state, more or less the creation of Lee Kuan Yew, who led the country with ruthless efficiency from 1959 to 1990 and was the world's longest serving Prime Minister (1965 to 1990). He was a strange mixture of authoritarian socialist and free marketeer. There is a high level of government spending on social services (though no soft-touch welfare support), producing, inter alia, a notably well educated and skilled population. At the same time Singapore is a major financial centre, one of the largest ports in the world and a significant exporter of manufactured goods, including petroleum products and electronic equipment.

One aspect that immediately strikes the visitor is the cleanliness of the city (the state is really no more than the city itself, though strictly speaking it consists also of a large number of very small islands). The buildings, streets and public spaces are invariably immaculate. Whereas in Hong Kong I would be inclined not to buy food from a street stall, in Singapore I had no such misgivings. I felt I couldn't spend three days there without drinking a gin sling at Raffles Hotel, but I found myself just one of many tourists trying and probably failing to conjure up the lost atmosphere of the original. History attracts the tourist, who then destroys it.

My hotel was one of many apparently similar establishments: large, modern, efficient, offering everything a guest could want and doubtless a few discreet oriental services which were not mentioned in the brochures and on the room lists. The hotel entrance gave onto a huge space that served many purposes. At the far end there was a long bar with enough stools to seat a rugby team but also plenty of room to form a scrum. Next there was an area of tables and chairs where tea or a light snack could be taken amongst the potted palm trees. Here, throughout the afternoon, a pianist would tinkle away at a grand piano, playing the same standard tea room repertoire that might equally have featured in such a setting fifty years earlier. Occasionally the pianist would be joined by a violin and a double bass to perform in a classic Palm Court style, encouraging a few brave couples to take to the floor, the whole affair thus blossoming into a genuine tea dance. In a 1980s concrete and glass building with every modern convenience, the hotel management were doing their best to create an ambience of the 1920s or 1930s. Nearer to the entrance was a lounge scattered with leather sofas and armchairs, an area always dimly lit and not particularly inviting unless you had a rendezvous you didn't wish to advertise, or you just wanted to snooze. Seated in the lounge was a group of people, a seemingly permanent fixture, who positioned themselves within a few yards of the main hotel lifts that were situated not far from the entrance. This can only have been deliberate, for they regularly addressed themselves to guests waiting for a lift, though I was never quite sure what they were saying or whether it might have been in some way offensive or provocative. I quickly decided that I should ignore any remarks tossed in my direction. Not that these people were threatening, but they certainly were distinctly odd. They were, to a man (or perhaps a woman), Indian in appearance and they were all either transvestites or transsexuals, husky voiced, invariably lavishly made up and dressed to the nines. That was all I learned about them. Their daily presence was and remains a complete mystery to me. Just another mystery of the Orient, to bamboozle the innocent westerner. But I wonder if Lee Kuan Yew approved.

Hiding In The Hills

In early 1996 I swapped the briefcase for the wheelbarrow. Instead of documents I carried soil, stones, gravel, sand and cement; taking the place of pens and calculators were shovels, spades, trowels, hammers and a chain saw. For the first time in my life I applied myself to serious manual work. This was DIY (do it yourself) with a vengeance; Helen referred to it more graphically as DYI (do yourself in).

Half a dozen years or so before this we had been on a motoring holiday in France, exploring some of the lesser known parts of the country and carefully avoiding tourist hotspots. We went to the Jura, where there are dramatic landscapes and historic fortified towns built from locally quarried stone many centuries ago. On a cobbled street in one of these towns we found a very fine lady's watch, which we handed in to the nearest police station. The duty officer took down our details, apparently not on an official form, and advised us that if the watch was not rightfully claimed within three months we would become the legal owners. Either way they would notify us of the outcome. Oh yes. I had a horrible feeling that the paper on which he had just written our names and address was in the bin almost before we had left the building. As we walked away I suggested to Helen that a policeman's wife might shortly receive a rather nice present from a generous husband. We heard no more of the matter. If the same thing happened again, would we react differently, perhaps less honestly?

With no particular plan in mind we looked at the map and discussed where we might head next. We settled for the Auvergne, a mountainous region in central France that I had long wanted to visit properly, having once passed through at great speed on my way from Cassis, near Marseilles, to Calais overnight with a friend in his Triumph TR4, a journey during which I drove faster than ever before or since, topping 110 miles an hour on the flat, straight, tree-lined roads of northern France. That was over forty five years ago now. Today I blanch at the thought of such recklessness and marvel that ordinary cars could reach such speeds in those far off days.

So we crossed to Puy de Dôme, a *département* with some of the most impressive peaks in the *massif central*. There we stayed in a modest hotel teeming with families on their annual summer holiday enjoying full board, which seemed to entail spending roughly half their time in the dining room, the other half being given over to just sufficient exercise to enable them to do justice to the next meal. There was a gramophone and alongside it a pile of records that people either put on themselves or requested a waitress to put on for them. Since that was where we were, I asked if they had *Chants d'Auvergne* by Canteloube. This brought only a blank look, which served me right for being a clever clogs. On the Puy de Sancy, at the foot of which our hotel lay, we learned our first lessons about walking in the mountains: set out with a good, detailed map, keep to defined routes and resist the temptation to take short cuts. Failing to observe these basic rules we found ourselves having to negotiate, first, a swamp that threatened to engulf us and secondly a series of deep ravines that shocked us by the suddenness of their appearance just yards ahead of us. It was an experience that was to stand us in good stead for the next several years.

From Pichérande in Puy de Dôme we meandered south until, in late afternoon, we started looking for a hotel for the night. One after another was full, in the little villages strung out along our route through the valleys running north to south between the craggy hills of the Cantal. Eventually, in some desperation since it was getting late, we telephoned the next hotel on our list, which we knew from the map to be on the other side of a high plateau, necessitating a long steep climb over a pass and an even longer, though more gentle, descent into an almost parallel valley. We were in luck: they had one room remaining which, with relief, we booked immediately.

We stayed three nights at the Hôtel de la Poste in Dienne, a small village at the lower end of a fertile valley, at an altitude of 1050 metres (3450 feet), the hills rising abruptly to about 1600 metres (5280 feet) on the plateau to the rear and sweeping up majestically to a rocky peak on the far side of the valley. Beyond that was the Plomb du Cantal, at 1855 metres (6120 feet) the highest point in the *département*. This was the start of something. For the next several years we returned to Dienne each summer to spend a week or ten days walking in the mountains, which we came to know and love. We became firm friends with the family who owned, and still own, the hotel and we visit them whenever we are in the area.

One year, it must have been 1995, we broke our habit to stay in a *gîte* a little further south, in the Lot. While there we looked at a couple of properties for sale, out of idle curiosity rather than with any particular intent. Neither of us expected our casual interest to evolve so quickly into a decision to buy; in fact I never thought of it as a decision, more something that simply happened, and in early 1996 we found ourselves taking possession of a former mill house in a remote valley 2000 feet up in the hills of the southern Cantal, about twenty-five kilometres south of the departmental capital, Aurillac.

The house itself was very modest, consisting of three rooms on two floors with an open staircase, off which was the later addition of a gloomy, low-ceilinged bathroom, where the damp entered so determinedly through the walls that we waged a constant war against a spreading, greenish black mould and the white enamel of the bath turned green in the space of a day or so. You could sit on the lavatory, in a curtained cubicle off the bathroom with no natural light, and listen to the mice scurrying playfully behind the boards with which the stone walls were crudely clad. Nevertheless, though there was limited scope for extension or major improvement short of knocking the place down and starting again from scratch, the house was quite habitable and, in only a short while, moderately comfortable. The real potential of the property lay outside.

The area of land was roughly one and a half acres. On this stood a huge barn on two floors, built on a steep slope so that each floor had its separate entrance at ground level. On the downside the high wall bulged alarmingly, while the wall on the top side was seriously concave and the roof, its timbers half rotted by the damp of many hard winters, sagged under the weight of its thousands of heavy old tiles. When the roof sprang a leak the remedy was to add more tiles to cover the hole, the effect being to increase the burden on the already overloaded rafters. The whole edifice seemed to be leaning, if not actually moving, centimetre by centimetre, inch by inch, down the side of the valley towards the house. Yet our friends the local *paysans* (small dairy farmers, as opposed to the huge agricultural businesses which produce grain and cereals on the flatter land in the north of France) said not to worry, it had probably been like that for the best part of two hundred years. This intended reassurance was of little comfort to me, since I reasoned that after a couple of centuries of continuous use and regular battering by mountain storms, the collapse of the barn must now be overdue. But, as always, the locals know best, and fifteen years later it has still not succumbed.

Tacked onto one end of the barn was another two storey building, one room up, one down, with no staircase nor even a ladder to connect the two, the upper part being accessed by a door giving onto the lane by which the *Moulin de Brayat*, for that was the name of the house, was approached. The lower room had been used as his workshop by a cabinet maker who had lived in the *moulin* with the lady from whom we bought the property and their young son, but a little while earlier he had died, when only in his forties, from a combination of alcohol and depression, though I am not sure which came first. To describe it as a workshop is rather flattering if not misleading, since it consisted of a rough workbench and two or three shelves on an earthen floor under a single dim electric light. The conditions notwithstanding, he produced some good quality furniture, somewhat heavy in the local style, which was then stored in the upper room until there was sufficient to hold a sale, which would be publicised by hand-written notices pinned up in neighbouring villages, with directions to the 'saleroom' indicated by arrows attached to trees on the lanes in the vicinity. The upstairs room was covered by a ceiling of shabby, badly worn fabric under a rusty corrugated iron roof, both of which had been installed as temporary measures some twenty years earlier. All the walls, inside and out, were of bare stone.

We decided to convert this building into a one bedroom *gîte*, to be let out during the summer months. The fact that we intended to create two new windows meant that we required planning permission, which presented no problem as we were welcome arrivals in the commune (and incidentally the only foreigners), we were providing work and putting money into the local economy, and the mayor was a very pleasant and helpful chap. He was one of several people who gave us advice on local artisans and we were soon able to select our team for the job.

The first thing I did was to call a meeting on site to agree a timetable for the work. Everyone turned up except the mason. Perhaps that shouldn't have mattered much but after a few minutes I began to suspect that his absence was calculated, because every time I tried to set start dates for those present they would say it all depended on the mason completing his work. So my attempt to fix and hold them to a defined programme fell at the first hurdle and I had to accept that it would be a piecemeal affair. None of our friends was surprised at this, but they assured us that everything would slot into place. And most of it did, after a fashion.

After a few alarms and much chasing, badgering

and cajoling, the *gîte*, which we called *L'Atelier* in recognition of its former function, was ready in time for
our first visitors in June 1999, some eighteen months
after work had begun.

In fact, just before the official inauguration, so to
speak, a golfing friend and his wife from Cambridge
had spent a week in the *gîte* as guinea pigs, to check
that everything was in order and to give us their views
on possible improvements to the arrangements we had
made. This plan failed on at least two counts. First, their
enjoyment of the holiday was somewhat undermined by
the weather. On their first day they decided to walk,
under clear skies, to the village to buy provisions. By
the time they got back several hours later they were not
only weary from the long steep climb, but burned to
a frazzle by the blistering sun. For the next six days it
rained incessantly. At the end of their week they were
able to report that they had identified thirty-one species of birds in the area, regretting that they had only
spotted twenty-eight, the remaining three having been
heard but not seen. Apart from an assurance that they
had found the *gîte* comfortable and well equipped, they
had no comment or suggestion to make. This was most
encouraging.

Seven days after their departure a civil servant and
his wife from Lincolnshire arrived, their estate car bursting with suitcases full of her outfits, which were more
appropriate to a couple of weeks at the Hôtel George
V in Paris than a week in a rural *gîte* in the Cantal. My
first duty was to rustle up every available additional coat
hanger, while apologising profusely (and insincerely)
for the inadequacy of the spacious double wardrobe
provided. Within hours there was a knock at our door.

Were we aware of the problem with the shower? The flow of water was fine, but after barely one minute ('my wife takes a great deal longer than that') it turned from hot to stone cold and no amount of adjustment to the controls could persuade it to heat up again.

The couple kindly volunteered that, since they were planning to spend the day in Aurillac, we could have unfettered access to the *gîte* to fix the shower during their absence. Behind this offer was the unspoken, yet unmistakable, threat that if things were not in order by the time they returned, we would be faced with a bill for reimbursement of our charges and the cost of alternative accommodation in hotels. By good fortune we managed to contact the plumber and impress upon him the extreme urgency of the situation, despite the fact that urgency did not normally feature in his vocabulary. He was quickly on site to make his diagnosis, all the while looking nervously at me as if awaiting a second opinion, as was his habit. There were to be times when I wished I had given him a second opinion first.

Anyway, the long and the short of it was that he had installed the water heater with the flue rising vertically, then turning at right angles to pass through the wall to vent its gases outside. Unfortunately these gases seemed unable or unwilling to go round corners, getting stuck at the bend and triggering some security feature that promptly switched off the boiler. The only solution was to redirect the flue straight upwards, thus allowing the gases unimpeded passage to the fresh air. This meant cutting holes in the ceiling, the roof lining and the tiles, while plugging the now redundant hole in the wall. Somehow all this was achieved before our guests arrived to dress for dinner, and if they appreciated our efforts they hardly showed it. When they left at the end of their week in the *gîte* they said it had been a relaxing break after the initial difficulties, but they kept themselves to themselves and I recall only one conversation, during which I enquired which branch of the civil service he worked in. 'I'm afraid I can't tell you that' he replied, effectively terminating the exchange and leaving me to wonder what sort of secrets they needed to hide in rural Lincolnshire.

Each summer for the next four years the *gîte* was fully booked and nearly all our visitors were most pleasant and thoroughly friendly. There was, of course, the odd exception. On one occasion our tenants were a lecturer in French at a north of England university and her boyfriend. They insisted on breaking the very few rules that we asked people to observe, such as not smoking indoors and not inviting *their guests* to stay overnight (there was only one bedroom). Whereas almost everybody made some effort to clean up before leaving, as requested, this couple left the place in a dreadful state, departing early in the morning without saying goodbye. We always invited visitors to our house for an aperitif on one evening during their stay, and it was just our bad luck that when this particular pair were having a glass of wine in our sitting room and conversation was flagging, a mouse scuttled across the floor at their feet and disappeared down a hole at the base of the wall. We tried to ignore it, but they were obviously alarmed and scuttled away themselves as soon as possible.

To my recollection, the only other disagreeable episode concerned a man of the cloth and his wife. The reverend gentleman, of uncertain denomination, seemed to be in a thoroughly bad humour when they arrived, declaring almost before he had seen inside, and definitely before they had unpacked the car, that the *gîte* was gloomy, dirty, and could not compare with the marvellous cottage in which they had stayed for the previous week. I took great exception to his complaint of dirtiness, since Helen in particular was meticulous about presenting the *gîte* in an immaculate state and our visitors' book was full of appreciative comments on the accommodation. Half addressing his wife and half aiming his remarks at me, he ranted on, saying that they should cancel their week's booking and leave immediately. Choosing my words carefully, I told him he was quite entitled to change his mind and that if he decided not to take up his reservation, that was entirely his affair and I, for one, would have no regrets. His wife tried to calm him, while settling the question of whether to go or stay by starting to unpack a couple of small bags. We avoided each other for the rest of the week in a most unchristian stand-off.

New guests were awaited on Saturday afternoons with a mixture of enthusiasm and trepidation. Once a couple failed to turn up, leaving us at something of a loss as to what, if anything, to do about it. The following morning we received a phone call to say that they were at a hotel twenty-five miles away and would not be coming to the *moulin*. When I enquired why this was, the chap said they had obeyed our directions to the letter, but had still got hopelessly lost, eventually deciding that they didn't want to stay somewhere so remote and hidden away that there was no guarantee of ever finding it again if they went out for the day.

On the basis that they had paid for their week and it seemed a pity to pay again for six more nights in hotels, I persuaded them that they should have another crack at finding us and carefully explained the simplest route. They pitched up an hour and a half later and were delighted with what they found.

That afternoon they asked me to recommend somewhere for dinner. 'A nice place,' they said, 'good food, never mind the price.' I suggested a hotel owned and run by a friend of ours, no more than a couple of miles away, an easy drive home and minimal risk of losing themselves on the way. Next morning they thanked me for a brilliant suggestion: they had enjoyed it so much that they had booked again for that evening. And, as it happened, for every other evening of their stay.

The bishop of Bristol came to relax for a week with his wife. On receiving their booking I had asked my brother if he knew him, since Jeff had been at the Cathedral School and was at the time President of the Old Cathedralian Society. He thought it better if I didn't mention the connection, since they had not always seen eye to eye. A couple were celebrating a special wedding anniversary, for which the wife may have acquired some new sexy underwear. Anyway, they made the mistake of leaving their front door open, which proved too great a temptation for Helen's dog Flynn, who turned up at the house looking very pleased with himself, with two pairs of fancy lace knickers in his mouth. At least one couple were so taken with the Auvergne that they bought a house higher up in the hills and moved there to live. Another, when they discovered the usual bottle of wine on the dining table (our welcoming gift), invited us to share it with them. During the course of a splendid afternoon together, they asked us to suggest a restaurant for a typical Sunday lunch the following day. We proposed a modest place in Maurs, a small town twelve miles to the south, which catered mostly for workmen during the week. There would be no menu and it didn't take bookings, so they should get there early to avoid disappointment, because it would be full in no time. Seeing them snoozing in the sun after their return, I decided to leave it a while before asking if they had enjoyed lunch at Maurs. 'Let me put it this way' said Mike, 'We won't be needing any dinner. After downing our first glass of wine, I poured us a second, raised my glass and said to Pat that I could think of nowhere in the world I would rather be at that moment. It was terrific.' Mike and Pat have remained good friends and visit us regularly in Beaugency, even though they now live in Queensland, Australia.

Our least welcome, and uninvited, guests were a family of pine martens, who lived in the nearby woods in the warmer weather but who took up residence for the winter in the space between the ceiling and the roof of L'Atelier. Of course they should never have been able to get in, but the builders somehow failed to close the gap at the top of one wall, so they could squeeze in under the eaves. The consequences of this were not catastrophic, just inconvenient, because it meant that every year, in the late spring, I had to treat and repaint the ceiling of the living room upstairs to cover over the stains caused by their careless toilet habits. Also upstairs, I managed to repel an uncharacteristically half-hearted invasion by a small gang of mice, who could normally be expected to eat their way through anything. Trapped between floors I can only suppose they simply expired, that is unless they just gave up, found an exit and decided there were richer and easier pickings elsewhere, such as down at our house.

One of the attractions of the *gîte* was the swimming pool, which we had built the year before we opened for business. It was of a very unusual design, notably in the fact that no plumbing was involved. For this reason many people were of the view that it couldn't possibly work, but it did, and well. The only minor disadvantage was that when the pool needed topping up, for example to compensate for evaporation, we had to run a hose from a nearby tap on the barn wall, which I suppose must have looked a bit rustic. At the deep end there was a unit, removable in its entirety for storage during the close season, containing an ingenious filtering system and a pump that sent a continuous stream of clean water round the pool, which was ovoid in shape, and finally sucked it back into the filter. You could thus say that the design was not only unusual but revolutionary. I used to hoover bottom and sides two or three times a week, so it was always immaculate. Anyway, the unanimous view of our guests, paying and non-paying, was that the pool was an absolute, sparkling gem and its setting, perched on the steep side of the valley, was both novel and inspirationally conceived.

On two sides we created a lawn and on the third we had a strong retaining wall built, four feet high and twenty inches thick, to ensure that we didn't wake up one morning after a storm to find that a part of the hillside had slipped quietly down into the pool. As with every other building project of ours, the stones for the wall were found on our plot, whether on or in the ground or in the Moulègre, the stream that runs down the valley and formerly drove the mill wheel.

One day I noticed that two or three large flat stones had been removed from an old existing wall and it was pretty obvious that they were being used to top off the new one, so I challenged the mason in charge of the work and, when he admitted his misdemeanour, made him put them back. We didn't quite fall out over this incident because the next morning when I went to greet the workmen the mason, nodding towards the house, asked if I had seen that the milkman had called. His apology for pinching the stones took the form of two rather good bottles of Bordeaux (I forget the precise *appellation*) which he had placed beside the doorstep.

At the shallow end you entered the pool by four semi-circular, so-called Roman steps. A couple of yards behind these was a flight of steps leading up to the pool-house, which served as changing room, storage space and nerve centre of the pool controls, that is to say a box on the wall, about six inches square, with an on/off switch and an automatic timer. This building had had a previous existence as a pigsty, the conversion of which started with the removal of an ancient deposit of pigshit, covering the earthen floor to a depth of nearly a foot and baked hard over the years. We installed three old windows where there had been doorways but no doors, and after relaying the roof tiles, putting down a concrete floor and giving the place a lick of paint, it fitted the bill perfectly. Just above the pool, behind the retaining wall, I levelled and grassed an area where there were loungers for those who preferred to spend their time, or some of it, less energetically than, say, hiking in the mountains or canoeing down the Lot, neither of which was far away. Above that I built a stone terrace, rather like a semi-circular stage, backed by an existing old wall, crescent shaped and serving I know not what original purpose. In my mind's eye I saw this little terrace being graced by a string quartet of beautiful young ladies playing Mozart, Beethoven or Schubert to a rapt audience around the pool. Alas, my grand vision never materialised, for which I have nobody to blame but myself, though whether a quartet of young lovelies, with or without the necessary instrumental skills, could have been found in the Cantal is another matter entirely. There, even among quite young girls, the ability to round up and milk a herd of cows would probably be more highly prized than perfect pitch or a fine bowing technique on the violin.

Not that we lived entirely without music. We did once go to a chamber concert at a chateau in the mountains a little way north of Aurillac, where a relatively sophisticated audience, evidently comprised mostly of holiday visitors, had gathered in some excitement to hear a rare visiting quartet. Even then it took place in a barn, albeit a splendidly restored barn, that was far too small to accommodate in anything approaching comfort the enthusiastic mass of music lovers who crowded in. Such was the press that we found ourselves practically deposited in the lap of the first violin, and you couldn't avoid feeling that their performance must have suffered in the circumstances. It can't have helped either that the temperature in that overpopulated barn was probably hovering in the upper thirties centigrade. On another occasion a friend was singing in a local choir that took part in a concert including Gabriel Fauré's beautiful Requiem, given at the oldest church in Aurillac. In the interval we crossed the road for a drink in a bar run by a former international rugby player, where from time to time there was singing of a different sort, unrehearsed and less delicate but more muscular, like the drinkers themselves.

Our nearest neighbour was about half a mile away from the *moulin*. My first encounter with her was probably as close as I ever came to engaging her in conversation. On a pleasantly warm spring evening I was doing something or other up by the barn when a figure approached soundlessly along the lane. As she drew closer I wished her a good evening, as I would any casual passer-by, for at that stage I had no idea who she might be.

'Have you seen my pig?' she enquired, 'I have lost my pig.'

If I gave an answer to this extraordinary question, then she certainly wasn't listening to it. She was ready with another: 'How much did you pay for the *moulin?*' I was naturally not prepared to respond to this impertinence, but moved a little closer to get a better look at this strange visitor. Her reaction was to back away, like a cornered animal. She was dressed in multiple layers from head to toe, the whole covered by some sort of plastic mackintosh, so dirty and greasy that its original colour could not easily be determined. Her head and most of her face were obscured by a heavy plastic bag apparently wrapped round and tied under the chin. The little that could be seen of her face and hands was coarse and clearly unwashed, probably not having been exposed to soap and water for many a moon, and offered no clue as to her age. In one hand she carried a scythe, in the other a long pitchfork.

She may have appeared so to the casual observer, but to describe Germaine as eccentric would be absurdly inappropriate, implying that her way of life was to some extent a conscious and deliberate choice. I know nothing of her family background, but she lived in one room of what was little more than a hovel on the hillside, surrounded by cats which reacted to human beings in just the same terrified way that she herself did; she seemed never to wash or change her clothes, whether it was the hottest of summer days or the coldest of winter nights; how she managed to feed herself remains a mystery, since she cultivated no land and had no means of getting to any shop, the nearest of which was several miles away; she was for ever in search of her mythical lost pig. Germaine died a lonely death, allegedly in her early sixties, mourned by few and quickly forgotten: a sad end to an immensely sad life, barely imaginable in the prosperous Europe of the second half of the twentieth century.

Germaine was most likely to have been the product of a consanguineous relationship ('we are all cousins here') and was one among many single people (*célibataires*) living out their adult lives alone or with siblings in the remote countryside of the Cantal. Another such was the chap who did the tiling in the *gîte*. He was apparently related to her, though less obviously a sad case, having the skills of a qualified artisan, being a meticulous, if slow, worker and by nature a social animal, always ready to down tools for a chat. Jean-Louis was of a mildly philosophical turn of mind, though not always fully capable of expressing himself with any fluency (with heavy irony, I called him *le petit philosophe*). He dabbled a bit in the subject of contemporary politics and, in the early days of the new labour government, seemed to be quite impressed by Tony Blair. At least he was rather pleased with himself for knowing the British Prime Minister's name. He was in the habit of talking to himself while he worked.

Running down the valley on the other side of the stream, not much more than a hundred yards from the *gîte*, was a single track railway line on which little one- or two-carriage trains passed perhaps three or four times a day on their short journey between Aurillac and Figeac, a bit further south in the Lot. On hearing a train, Jean-Louis would invariably cry out '*TGV, Boisset à Paris*', then, as a complete non sequitur and for no reason that

I could ever discern, at the top of his voice, 'Tony Blair'. The best I can offer is that somehow, in his tortuous mind, the vigorous young PM was inextricably coupled with the surging technology of the *Train à Grande Vitesse*. At a stretch he might have claimed a metaphorical link, but I suspect in reality the juxtaposition was rather more haphazard. On one occasion I went to his house for some reason concerning the work on the *gîte*, and he invited me in for a glass of cheap white wine in his kitchen. It looked as if this was the only room in the house in use, since there was a bed in one corner and a television that he could watch from his place at the table. He had lived all his life in this house and still spoke with great sadness of the loss of his parents and the pain caused by their absence, despite the fact that they had died many years earlier and he was now in his fifties. On a return visit to the area a couple of years ago we bumped into him heading home on a tractor. He had aged hugely in the few intervening years and was clearly the worse for wear from alcohol in mid-afternoon. The likelihood is that he found nothing to occupy him in his retirement and had taken to the bottle. Another sad end beckoned to a narrowly limited existence.

I had once asked him if he had ever been abroad.

'Yes,' he had replied, 'I went to Marseilles during national service in the Army. I didn't like it.'

'And is that it?' I continued, ignoring his interesting concept of what constituted abroad.

'No,' he said, 'I once went to Paris for a day.'

'What did you think of Paris?'

'I hated it.'

Life in the country can sometimes be idealised. There is another side to that coin.

In the interest of painting a reasonably balanced

picture, it should be said that some of the artisans who worked on the *gîte* were almost normal. I have already said that at least the tiler, whatever his other oddities, was pretty good at his job. So too the mason when he put his mind to it, though he could be obstinate to the point of pigheadedness and spent rather too much time acting the pompous President of the local wild boar hunt. For his generally bossy attitude we dubbed him *le petit Napoléon*. The carpenter was fairly dependable, despite losing a brother during the project to an accident in which he failed to take a sharp bend, careered off the road and plunged down an almost vertical slope for several hundred feet. The roofer was conscientious, skilful and quick, with the build and reactions of a high-flying acrobat, which I sometimes felt he could be as he moved nimbly on the edge of a vertiginous drop to the ground.

Then there was the plumber. He was a rather weedy looking chap whose blue overalls were usually undone almost to the waist, revealing a pale, hairless chest which would have been better covered. When asked a question he would normally reply with practised ambiguity, all the while looking at you quizzically as if to say 'well, what do you think?' and waiting for you to take the lead. One way and another we were obliged to call on his services quite a lot during our seven years at the *moulin* and he never really let us down.

Once we had a problem with the lavatory, which was blocked and remained so despite our vigorous attempts to clear it. The plumber arrived and repeated the treatment to no avail, water levels now threatening to flood the bathroom. After some thought and much shilly-shallying, he went outside, located the waste pipe and drilled a small hole in the top at a point close to the back wall. The result was a vertical spurt of water, rather as one pictures the striking of oil. Having resealed the pipe with a blob of cement, he moved along a bit and repeated the process, with precisely the same outcome. After making four holes, each of which produced the same gush of water, thus demonstrating that the blockage must be further downstream, so to speak, he had more or less reached the septic tank (*fosse septique*) into which the pipe disgorged its contents. Here his eyes lit up and he exclaimed, with a note of something close to triumph in his voice, that he had cracked the problem. Casually dislodging the obstruction with a stick that lay on the ground nearby, he declared the flow from the pipe to be restored and at a stroke normal service was resumed. I was rather annoyed with him for being such a dope (it can't have been the first time he had encountered just such a problem), but in truth I was angrier with myself for not having given a bit more thought to the matter and for not realising from the outset that the search for the blockage must logically start at the far end and work back towards the lavatory. As on other occasions when my first instinct might have been to grasp the plumber warmly by the throat, I desisted and limply thanked him for sorting things out. Who knows, one day he might be needed to extricate us from a real fix. And anyway, I couldn't help quite liking the poor soul.

I have already made reference to the presence of mice in the *moulin*, one having scampered across the room at the very feet of a couple we had invited to join us for an aperitif, others scurrying around in the walls of the bathroom. They were to be found, I suspect, in all old houses in the countryside and they were quite impossible to eliminate. I fed them a regular diet of the strongest rat poison available from retail outlets, but either they learned to avoid it, in which case some other creature was tucking in because it certainly disappeared, or they developed a resistance, perhaps even an immunity, that enabled them to eat it with no ill effects. For all I know they enjoyed the stuff, looked forward to a second helping. I also blocked every hole, every possible means of entry or exit I could find, with a generous filling of cement, but to no avail. They always found a way, though strangely there was never a trace of a mouse upstairs. Nor were there ever any rats in the house.

Outside, though not in the immediate vicinity of the house, there were ground rats. You never saw them, but the evidence of their existence was clear in the holes from which I assume they emerged at night. We had quite a lot of something that the locals called a *rat taupier* (a mole-like rat), which lived underground, but not by much, constructing its galleries just below the surface so that its passage was marked by a line of raised turf. This was not only unsightly because this particular rodent ate the roots, thus killing the grass above, but it was also inconvenient since if you inadvertently stepped on the raised area, you could easily turn your ankle as your foot sank through the gallery roof. I have mentioned these so-called *rats taupiers* to any number of friends in different parts of France and so far have never found anybody who has even heard of them. They do not put in an appearance in either of my English-French dictionaries, which list a total of thirteen different sorts of rat, admittedly not all of which are strictly of the burrowing variety: *rat de bibliothèque*, for example, does not mean a rodent in residence at the library, but a bookworm. Maybe nobody outside the Cantal makes a distinction between them and ordinary ground rats (if indeed these exist as a species) or between them and moles.

Now, the subject of moles is one on which I am fairly knowledgeable, albeit not in any zoological sense. They had a nasty habit of invading and marching across our modest patch of land, from time to time shovelling up the displaced earth from their galleries to make a mess of what otherwise could almost pass for a lawn in front of the house. For my part, I did everything in my power to hunt them down, repel them, catch them or mount some form of effective counter-attack. They were far too clever for me. They were also too smart for the manufacturers of anti-mole products, for which I scoured the hardware shops and the garden centres for miles around. So many different devices were available that it was obvious no single solution was up to the job. As far as I can remember, I started my campaign with poison. It may be that one or two succumbed to this, but if so I never found the proof. Of course they may have staggered off to warn their friends and to die in the bosom of their families. On a few occasions I took the fight directly to the enemy. Happening on a new mole-hill in the course of its creation, the builder, though not itself visible, furiously shovelling the earth from below, I seized a garden fork and repeatedly thrust it down at various points through the loose upturned soil in a frenzied assault. Activity ceased. Aha, success at last. I dug down and there were the galleries to right and left, but the blessed beast had bolted.

Next I tried a device designed not to kill the moles but to drive them away, *chez les voisins*, assuming you had some. This was a product conceived and born of a marriage of pure optimism with wild fantasy. It consisted of a baton about eighteen inches long with a small battery in the base. You buried it to a depth of six inches or so and the upper half emitted radio waves undetectable by humans but devastating to the subterranean visitors, who would flee the area as fast as their little webbed feet would carry them. I purchased two and installed them in strategic positions. That afternoon while I was out our friend Michel came to mow the back field. We had a mutually beneficial arrangement whereby he gained a bale or two of hay for winter feed for the cows, and we kept a neat and orderly back field in the holiday months without any effort on our part. It didn't occur to me that my new toys might be in the firing line. As it happened I had planted them close to where the mown lawn gave way to the wild grass, just in range of the big mowers pulled by Michel's tractor as it swept round the outer edges of the field. My magic sticks were cleanly shorn off about three inches above the ground, having been in place a mere couple of hours.

'Never mind', said Michel. 'They wouldn't have worked anyway.'

I'm sure he was right. Finally, I opted for snaring the moles and equipped myself with a dozen traps, which had to be laid in pairs at the entrances to a gallery on either side of the access hole I had dug (usually below a molehill), because I couldn't know which way the animal would come sauntering along. I had two or three encouraging early successes, but somehow it seemed to become more and more difficult to persuade the enemy into my ambushes. Had they got wise to me or had it been a case of beginner's luck? I ensnared a few more, enough to feel that I had won the odd battle, but there was no disguising the fact that I had lost the war.

Life in the Cantal was not confined to the struggle against nature, and was by no means all work – there was plenty of play too. August 15th, the Feast of the

Assumption, is a public holiday (*jour férié*) in France, where incidentally there are roughly twice as many as in England. (The month of May, for example, hardly figures as a working month because there are three public holidays, each of which is commonly 'bridged' to the preceding or following weekend to make several additional consecutive days off.) The first year we were there we had a party at the *moulin*, to which all the friends we had made locally were invited. In theory it was lunch, but in fact it went on for the rest of the day. Everyone was terrifically generous, bringing home-cooked dishes or salads or cheese (one friend was Director of the local creamery where they made the famous Cantal cheese, so we ate only the very best), and one or two bottles of wine each. A good time was had by all and as a result it became a fixture in the calendar each year.

Once half a dozen English friends came over to celebrate Helen's birthday, a rather special one, and we arranged various outings and events to mark the occasion. One such was a dinner party in a private room at a hotel in a village about fifteen kilometres away, where we had got to know the owners quite well, the husband being an excellent chef and the wife a welcoming hostess. To this party we invited six French friends to match the number of English guests. It is fair to say that the French, being country folk, spoke barely a word of English between them, while several of the English had at least a smattering of French. The wine greatly assisted the process of breaking down barriers and it was not long before everyone was in animated conversation, regardless of whether any of it was being understood.

It is said that a little knowledge is a dangerous thing, and that is certainly true of language: recognising an odd word or phrase without understanding the context can cause a leap to entirely the wrong conclusion. An English member of the party asked her neighbour at table what she did for a living, to which Francine replied '*Je suis infirmière psychiatrique*'. Picking up, as she thought, '*je suis fermière*', Rosamond proceeded to explore every aspect of the farm run by Francine and her husband. 'Did they have cows? How many? What sort of cows? And sheep? Chickens? How much land did they farm? Did they grow crops? What sort of crops? Was it very difficult farming such hilly terrain?' Whatever the answers to all these questions, Rosamond was not to be deterred. She had the bit between her teeth. For her part, Francine was increasingly bemused at this line of questioning, but found it hard to bring the misunderstanding to a head.

Later, she explained to me what had happened and how they had been talking at cross purposes. Fortunately I was able to put my finger on the source of the confusion. When I told Rosamond that she had impressed with her French, but that in one respect she had got slightly the wrong end of the stick and that Francine was not a farmer, nor even a farmer's wife, but a psychiatric nurse, she took it in good part and laughed nearly as much as everyone else. In a way, this forgivable little misapprehension helped to make the whole evening a great success. Everybody entered into the spirit.

There were other parties. On the only occasion we were down at the *moulin* at the year end, we were invited to dinner on New Year's Eve. There were about a dozen of us and we were all awash with champagne long before sitting down to eat at perhaps ten o'clock. Everyone brought a dish or in some cases a whole course. Christine, asked to provide something as a starter, turned up with scores of oysters, snails in garlic by the bucketful and heaps of *jambon d'Auvergne*, the local cured ham. And all the rest of the guests were equally generous, so dinner took on the proportions of a mediaeval banquet, with all the extravagance of such feasts, at least in the popular imagination. Helen made two desserts, each sufficient to serve twelve decent helpings. After the sherry trifle had been passed round, appetites were pretty much sated and still half the bowl remained untouched. 'Would anyone like some more of this?' enquired our host, holding up the dish, nameless because it had never before been encountered by the French. Receiving no positive response, he took this as *carte blanche* to demolish all that remained of the trifle, which he did with a broad smile of appreciation on his face. Helen had an instant convert to *la cuisine anglaise*.

Invitations to meals with friends were by no means a rarity, often being impromptu affairs, either because we just happened to be passing or when aperitifs stretched unplanned into dinner. It was always a pleasure, no matter how simple the fare. Food is of course near to the heart of every French person, and the word *manger* is probably the most used verb in the language apart from *être* and *faire*. We would buy as much of our food as possible from the market each Thursday morning in Maurs, a small town about twelve miles away to the south. The market was a very social gathering, where you were guaranteed to bump into any number of friends, so one or two glasses in the teeming bars of the circular main street were more or less obligatory. And one or two glasses often turned into lunch on the terrace at La Grande Fontaine, and who would contemplate lunch without a glass or two of wine?

The delights of summer in the Cantal when the weather was good were almost infinite: walking on our favourite peaks, the hillsides covered in wild flowers, with free-roaming ponies and fleet-footed mountain deer as common sights, along with the majestic buzzards wheeling soundlessly in the vastness of the clear blue skies. Tired from our strenuous hike we would sometimes drop in to a beautifully restored house, at the top of the highest hamlet for miles around, the summer home of two friends, retired Paris academics, where Serge would be lovingly tending his garden and Michèle would make tea and serve delicious home-made cake. She was a larger than life character in every respect and could talk the hind legs off a donkey, but they were, and are, an absolutely charming couple.

In the other direction was the Lot, a river of serious proportions and many moods, though mostly benign. There were a few stretches of shallow, rock-strewn white water that could test the modest skills of any inexperienced canoeist. One year my step-daughter Sidonie, then still a teenager, brought a friend on holiday to the *moulin* and we went canoeing. They insisted on their own separate boat and were doing well until they reached the first set of rapids, where they immediately came a cropper. The canoe overturned, throwing them both into the water. A ducking didn't matter much, but they managed to lose several items of clothing, sunglasses and one or two other bits and pieces. Recovery was made more difficult by the fact that they were convulsed with laughter, as their canoe made off swiftly downstream on its own. They, the boat and the situation were rescued in the nick of time by a couple of lads of about their age who happened to be shooting past at that very moment.

In search of less energetic pursuits we would sometimes go to Figeac, a beautiful little town in the Lot, perhaps on market day when the place hummed with activity and the cafés were bursting with life.

Alternatively, we might have a day out at a village such as the mediaeval Conques, perched high on the cliffs above a tributary of the Lot, which has its own music festival of chamber and choral works performed in the magnificent setting of its renowned abbey church, where you feel yourself transported to another age. Not far from Conques is the resort town of Entraygues, where the rushing waters of the Truyère descend from its steep-sided gorges to the north east to converge with the Lot, which arrives from the south east and flows west, via Cahors and Villeneuve, all the way to Aiguillon, where it joins forces with the mighty Garonne, which only gives way to the Gironde just before entering the Atlantic north of Bordeaux.

On the way home from Entraygues we might pass through the pretty village of Montsalvy, source of a delicious soft cheese, and finally stop for a beer in the circular-walled village of Marcolès, which has attracted a number, if not a school, of artists, whose work is displayed for sale in several galleries lining the old main street. We could even extend our tour, taking a slight *déviation* to Aurillac, the capital of the Cantal. It is also referred to by some as *la capitale du parapluie*, and with some reason, for it does seem to rain rather a lot. But it is a town of considerable charm, with some fine old churches, a handsome central square and a maze of pedestrian lanes full of cafés, bars and unusual boutiques. It is easy to forget that this is a small town of just 35,000 people, until you raise your eyes and see that at the end of every main street the green hills climb abruptly, ensuring that there can be no suburban sprawl here.

Many French regard the Cantal as a lost territory, by which they mean that it is completely off the beaten track and mired in an age perhaps forty or fifty years behind the rest of the country. While this may be true and may condemn the whole area in the eyes of the sophisticates, it is at the same time a part of its attraction to those seeking an escape from the pace and pressures of modern urban life. After all, what could be more calming than to draw back your curtains in the morning and look out on a lovely green landscape populated by nothing but a lazy herd of *Salers Rouges*, the distinctive reddish-brown cows that are such a feature of the Cantal countryside. (One farmer we knew well came to his retirement, unwisely sold his herd and was so bereft and heartbroken that he died within months.) With its craggy, sharp peaks rising to well over six thousand feet, its gentler rolling hills dotted with isolated farmhouses and tiny clustered hamlets, and its plunging wooded valleys, there is no doubting the extreme natural beauty of the place.

The Cantal is beautiful, but it is also sad, partly on account of its isolation, its backwardness, its relative poverty in a largely prosperous country, partly because its people have until recently been reluctant to move away from their roots, resulting in a closed community, often suspicious of outsiders, and a degree of local intermarriage that may be worthy of anthropological study. True, it is changing now, but slowly.

Within the last decade a book was published with the title of *Pays Perdu* (Lost Country). The event was not exactly sensational and the best-seller lists were undisturbed by its arrival in the nation's bookshops. Yet in one small corner of France it caused a real rumpus. The author was Pierre Jourde, a lecturer at the University of Grenoble. Though born on the outskirts of Paris, he had grown up in a small, remote village in the Cantal.

Now he wrote about the life and the people of this village, disguising it, its precise location and the identities of its inhabitants in what was billed as a work of fiction. Far from being a fond recollection of life in deepest rural France, nor yet a work of the imagination that just happened to be set there, it was seen as a withering account of that life and everything about it, including the harshest of caricatures of those who peopled it. The book came to the attention of the villagers and when, shortly afterwards, the author paid a visit to the area, he was physically attacked by the furious locals who felt they had been cruelly and cynically traduced. Worse, they had been betrayed by one of their own.

Yet, however exaggerated, to anyone familiar with that part of the world it painted a sadly recognisable picture. There is a saying that has been applied to the Cantal, though it seems doubtful that it would have originated there: *le corbeau vole sur le dos pour ne pas voir la misère* (the crow flies on its back to avoid seeing the poverty below).

These tensions being acknowledged, our sojourn in the Cantal was mostly fun and often funny. I can't help feeling that the following incident could only have happened there. On our way home from Maurs one day we were stopped for exceeding the speed limit. As I stepped out of the car the two gendarmes clicked their heels and gave me a smart salute, which I could barely resist returning. (I thought of Sir Robert Boothby visiting Hitler before the war. He was marched in and presented to the German leader, who, instead of shaking hands, leapt to his feet and gave the Nazi salute, crying 'Hitler', to which the Englishman replied in like manner, crying 'Boothby'.)

They admonished me briefly and demanded to see

my driving licence, of which I only had a photocopy. This bemused them, so they asked for my insurance document. I passed it over and watched as they scrutinised it, turning it this way and that, even attempting to read it upside down.

Eventually they gave up and dismissed me with a warning and another sharp salute. I had a funny feeling about that insurance document, so when we got home I fished it out again. It was ten months out of date.

The French Mistress

I suppose I must have been standing there gazing out of the front window for a minute or two, half daydreaming but half watching the chap opposite cutting his hedge. Imposing a little order on nature is something which occupies me from time to time at home, where things can't be allowed to get too far out of control in the restricted area of our mostly paved courtyard. My job is the essentially practical one of pruning the bushes, trees and prickly wall-climbing species so that light and air can reach the flower beds below, where the more creative business of choosing and arranging the plants is my wife Helen's concern. I like to put a bit of shape into this pruning though my efforts fall well short of qualifying as topiary. At the mill-house in the Auvergne where we used to spend long summers we felt the pool was a little exposed so I planted a laurel screen, to which I regularly took the shears to curb its over-exuberant growth, and at a certain point I discovered that I had inadvertently coaxed it into the form of a dragon *couchant*. From that moment on visitors were invited to admire the beast and were increasingly permitted, perhaps even tacitly encouraged, to believe that what had been a pure accident was in fact the result of deliberate, creative design.

My reverie was interrupted by a passing lady tennis player, immaculate in her whites, her short skirt maximising the effect of long brown legs. I thought of Miss Joan Hunter Dunn and wondered if this girl too was off to the club to meet, and beat, her own besotted subaltern. I then left the house on some trivial shopping errand and mentioned none of this to the neighbour. He had just finished his work and was tidying away the clippings from the pavement, so I crossed the road to congratulate him on the neatness of his hedge, with its now ruler-straight sides and razor-sharp edges.

'Well, that's very kind of you to say so. Thank you,' he said, 'but I'm not sure how long I can go on doing it myself. I'm eighty now you know.'

'Oh, come on, I'd say you look fit as a fiddle. If you paid some odd job man to trim it for you, he'd never produce such a professional finish.'

'Maybe not, but I am eighty.'

'You'd be dissatisfied and probably end up redoing it yourself. I saw an old fellow, older than you I swear, cutting that hedge over there the other day. And just look at the state of it! He was obviously doing it for a bit of extra money, had no pride in the job and didn't even bother to clear up the cuttings. Anyway, I reckon the exercise helps keep you young.'

'You may be right' he conceded, and after a pause he added 'You're over from France, aren't you? I noticed the car. We know Helen of course.' Obviously deciding that my confirmation of the facts was unnecessary, he continued 'I've got fond memories of France. We've been there many times on holiday, in different parts of the country, but originally I was there in the Army.'

'Oh, really.' I did a quick calculation: aged eighty, so born in 1929 and therefore aged only sixteen at the end of the war. 'Would that have been national service, or were you a regular soldier?'

'No, no. I was more of a bookworm. A career in the military would never have suited me. It was just national service. I was called up in 1955.'

Another bit of mental arithmetic. 'My gosh.' I was genuinely surprised. 'That was only two years before me. You had a very late call-up.'

'Yes, I was twenty-six, a lot older than most recruits. I kept being deferred because I was studying full time, but they got me in the end. Not that I minded. I had a jolly good time in the Army.'

'I think a lot of people did, in their different ways. I certainly did myself.'

'Hmm. In my case it was quite a strange business. For a start I was called up ten days before I was due to get married. When I told them that all the wedding arrangements had been made – the church booked, reception all paid for and everything ready to go – they were very decent about it. Mind you, what else could they have done? I wasn't too happy being married looking like a squaddie with my military short back and sides, but at least they gave me compassionate leave for the wedding and a few days' honeymoon, though we had no time to go away. Then I was posted to Aldershot and after basic training I became a driver in the Signals Corps.'

'Was that interesting?' I asked in all innocence, but it was the spur he needed.

'Not especially. On the other hand it gave me a lot of freedom and transport wasn't too much of a problem.' He laughed. 'The best thing was that I got on very well with my boss, who was a major. We had interests in common.'

'What sort of interests were they, if you don't mind

my asking?' I expected no more than a fairly standard list: books, music, sport, that sort of thing. Maybe snooker or table tennis, the things people occupy themselves with on Army camps, to keep boredom at bay.

'Mainly that we were both keen collectors of pictures, photographs of girls, women. Porn really, I suppose. We collected the kind of pictures you found in what people used to call dirty magazines. Remember, you didn't find them displayed openly on newsagents' shelves in those days. It was definitely under the counter stuff. Anyway, I seemed to be better at getting my hands on them than he was, so he was pretty much in my debt. But we were good chums and when I was posted to France we corresponded and continued to exchange pictures, though the traffic was mostly one way, because there were a lot more magazines of that sort available in France.'

'So where were you stationed in France?' I enquired, wondering now what further revelations might be about to be unveiled. Or perhaps I might be invited inside to cast an eye over his collection.

'Near Versailles. Luckily this meant that I could get into Paris quite easily. The major was very happy because there were all manner of pornographic magazines available in Paris and I could send them to him by secure internal post so there was no risk of interception or censorship. It worked well.'

'Did you know the left bank? I'm thinking particularly of a place I discovered in 1956, which must have been during your time over there. La Cave de la Huchette (or was it Le Caveau?) in St Germain – it was a jazz club buried deep below some cheap and cheerful bistro in Rue de la Huchette. What was then known as the Latin quarter.'

'I certainly did. When I was young I was very keen on traditional jazz. I remember listening to Stephane Grappelli there. My one regret was that I never heard him playing with Django Reinhardt and the Hot Club de France quintet, because of course Django was dead by then. But it was great stuff, and a marvellous atmosphere. What I'd call a respectable dive, don't you think?'

'A good description. I was not yet eighteen when I was there and it was all very exciting. Well, you do seem to have enjoyed yourself. At least when you weren't working.'

'You bet I did. And of course I had a mistress in Paris. Funnily enough, that was the greatest danger I faced in my brief Army career and, in a sense, my proudest military achievement, because she was also the mistress of a French general. We shared her, which didn't worry me, but whereas I knew all about him, fortunately he didn't know I even existed. Things had to be managed pretty carefully so as not to jeopardise the *entente cordiale*, but even then there were a few close shaves. A bit too close for comfort actually. Not quite a case of hiding in the wardrobe, but not far off either. She used to laugh at these alarms, though it was only in retrospect that I could see the funny side: I think she must have got more of a kick than I did out of near-disaster. Perhaps that's why she entertained us both – living dangerously with the two extremes of the military hierarchy – but who was taking the risk? I sometimes wondered how the general might have reacted to the discovery that he was sharing his mistress with a Signals driver. A Gallic shrug? Pistols at dawn? Or the ultimate *crime passionnel*?'

The question was left hanging in the scented air of an early summer morning on a very English suburban street as I strolled off to buy the bread and other bits and pieces, while my gentle neighbour, devoted father of five, retired publisher and lover of French culture, went inside for a nice cup of tea with his wife of fifty-four years.

Last Word

This has nothing to do with autobiography or geography. It may be entirely apocryphal. But, for my money, it's a fitting little anecdote to bring this ramble to a close.

Travels with a briefcase need not necessarily involve great distances and, as we have seen, the briefcase may in some instances have been notional or non-existent. I accept that it is highly unlikely that a Secretary of State in His Majesty's Government in the 1920s, or for that matter at any other time, would have burdened himself with a briefcase on his daily stroll from home in Mayfair to Westminster and back. A stout Malacca cane or a furled umbrella would have suited his needs to perfection.

In any event, the story goes that F E Smith (later 1st Earl of Birkenhead) fell into the habit of popping in to the Athenaeum to relieve himself on his way home from the Houses of Parliament in the evening.

After a while this was brought to the notice of the Secretary by a member who objected to such presumption, however elevated the status of the offender. On the occasion of his next visit, the Secretary was waiting for him and challenged him thus:

'I must point out, Sir, that you have no right to the

use of these facilities, since you are not a member of this club.'

'Good God,' replied F E Smith, 'do you mean to say this is a club as well?'

Lightning Source UK Ltd.
Milton Keynes UK
19 January 2011
165974UK00001B/26/P